CELEBRATION OF HAND-HOOKED RUGS XXI
2011 Edition

Editor
Debra Smith

Author
Ayleen Stellhorn

Designer
CW Design Solutions, Inc.

Circulation/Advertising Coordinator
Gail Weaverling

Magazine Assistant
Candice R. Derr

Operations Manager
Anne Lodge

Publisher
Judith Schnell

*Rug photographs provided by the artist
unless otherwise noted.*

Rug Hooking magazine is published five times a year in Jan./Feb., March/April/May, June/July/Aug., Sept./Oct., and Nov./Dec. by Stackpole, Inc., 5067 Ritter Road, Mechanicsburg, PA 17055. *Celebration of Hand-Hooked Rugs* is published annually. Contents Copyright© 2011. All rights reserved. Reproduction in whole or part without the written consent of the publisher is prohibited. Canadian GST #R137954772.

NOTICE: All patterns and hooked pieces presented here are Copyright© the individual designers, who are named in the corresponding captions. No hooked piece presented here may be duplicated in any form without the designer's consent.

A Publication of

R·U·G HOOKING

5067 Ritter Road
Mechanicsburg, PA 17055
(717) 796-0411
(877) 462-2604
www.rughookingmagazine.com
rughook@stackpolebooks.com

ISBN-978-1-881982-76-0

Printed in U.S.A.

Introd

Celebration *creates a dialogue about rugs. Most all our fiber artists get the book and we talk about this rug or that, a special background, the way one of the artists treated a face, the explosion of color in a rug. We become better at what we do because we have this book of wonderful rugs to ponder.*—Sharon Townsend

Celebration *is like scanning the world for the best inspiration in rug hooking. It chronicles what is happening in the contemporary landscape and creates new stepping stones to the future of our craft and art.*—Bea Brock

As a collector, I love to make connections with the past. We owe it to future generations to share the history of our works of art!
—Cynthia Norwood

Rug hookers have collected Celebration *issues over the last 20 years and rely on them for inspiration and insight into the artists' use of techniques, designs & colors.*—Kathy Wright, Sauder Village Rug Hooking Week

Rug Hooking proudly presents the finalists of our twenty-first annual *Celebration of Hand-Hooked Rugs* competition. Each September, we eagerly await the entries to see the new pieces, and each year we are dazzled and delighted by your wonderful creations. This year is no exception—the competition was tough and the rugs are simply amazing.

This annual publication is important in the world of rug hooking and in the larger world of textile arts. It presents an overview of some of the best work of the past year by some of the best hookers, be they well-known hookers that we have watched develop through the years or new names and new talents—people with a new vision and a different approach. Whether these new names are pushing the boundaries with intriguing techniques or hooking our favorite old patterns from years gone by, we are thrilled to see their work.

The *Celebration* competition and annual book is important in another way. It documents and preserves your pieces for generations to come. Decades from now—perhaps even into the next century—textile artists, your descendents, and all who love beautiful work will see these masterpieces. Each linen-and-wool hooked piece can only ever be in one place, and we know that all of these rugs will have long lives in the homes of people who love and appreciate them. But the finalists found in the pages of *Celebration* will have an additional life—in these books that are recognized as one of the finest collections of hooked rugs ever. Rugs in a book are immortal and will be seen and celebrated worldwide. What a great legacy—and we are honored to present them to you and to the world each year.

So settle back and enjoy the year 2010 in the world of rug hooking. Be inspired and delighted. The rugs and the rug hookers deserve our admiration.—*Debra Smith*

On the Cover: Van Gogh's Twelve Sunflowers, *Sally Kerr. Read more about her rug on pages 104–105.*

Table of Contents

page 36

page 66

page 102

Meet the Judges

Each year, four rug hooking artists and teachers judge the *Celebration* entries. Now that the competition is online, our judges can "travel" digitally to view the nearly 200 entries. This newfound geographical diversity is an asset to the competition. The *Celebration* rugs come from everywhere; now the judges do as well, bringing their diverse backgrounds and skills to the competition. This year they hailed from Ontario, Vermont, Michigan, and Texas. They judged from the comfort of their own homes, taking all the time they needed to thoughtfully and carefully consider the merits of each rug.

They are renowned teachers, artists, inspired colorists, award-winning hookers, businesswomen, and mentors. Their approaches to rug hooking and design are varied and comprehensive, encompassing everything from the most traditional to the most eclectic styles. They are an inspiring group of women who know the hooking world and are eminently qualified to judge the *Celebration* rugs. We are pleased and honored that they agreed to serve as judges in our twenty-first year.

Susan Quicksall
Oglesby, Texas

Susan has been designing and teaching various needle arts for more than 25 years. She owns Holly Hill Designs, a rug hooking pattern design and hand-painted needlepoint design business, which she started in 1980 and named after her daughters Holly and Hillary. She is a former graphic designer and interior decorator.

Susan's work has been featured in *Rug Hooking* magazine, *The American Profile* magazine, *ATHA newsletter*, *RHM's Celebration X, XI, XII, All Time Favorites*, and *Designs for Primitive Rug Hookers*. She wrote a dye formula/swatch book, *Dyeing For Color*, maintains a website, and operates a studio in McGregor, Texas. She is an accredited McGown instructor and a member of the Association of Traditional Hooking Artists (ATHA). She is self-taught and has been hooking and designing since 1995.

Jeanne Field
Aurora, Ontario, Canada

Jeanne has been hooking for 47 years and teaching for 44 years. She owns and operates a rug hooking business called Rittermere-Hurst-Field. Jeanne designs patterns and teaches across Canada and occasionally in the United States. She is a member of the Ontario Hooking Craft Guild (OHCG); ATHA in the United States; and a founding member of the International Guild of Handhooking Rugmakers (TIGHR).

She wrote *Shading Flowers* (Stackpole, 2006), and has written articles for *Rug Hooking* magazine. She also produced a 55-minute DVD called "Let's Hook," which provides beginners with an introduction to rug hooking. Jeanne has four children. All are grown and show great interest in the hooking community. Her own passion for the art form encourages others to take up and explore this wonderful art.

Stephanie Allen-Krauss
Montpelier, Vermont

Stephanie was only six when she learned to hook from her mother, Anne Ashworth, a nationally recognized rug hooking teacher and custom-dye specialist. This family tradition began with Stephanie's great-grandmother, Philena Moxley, who created and stamped embroidery and rug patterns at her shop in Lowell, Massachusetts, from 1865 to1882.

As a fourth generation rug hooker, Stephanie learned to dye wool fabric as a teenager and then to repair antique hooked rugs in her early twenties as a stay-at-home mom. For twenty years, she helped her mother with Green Mountain

Rug School, an annual event at Vermont Technical College in Randolph Center, where more than 200 rug hookers from all over the United States, Canada, and England meet for classes each June. In 2000, when her mother retired, Stephanie accepted the directorship of that school, and a decade later, she opened Fall Foliage Fiesta, another annual rug hooking school located on the campus of Vermont College of Fine Arts in Montpelier.

Stephanie owns and operates Green Mountain Hooked Rugs, a retail shop in Montpelier, Vermont, where she offers a wide variety of supplies for rug hookers. Stephanie hooks commission rugs and continues to repair rugs and do custom dyeing. She also offers classes and occasionally travels around the country to teach.

She is a past vice president of the Green Mountain Rug Hooking Guild, and was the treasurer for TIGHR. In 2010, Stephanie received the Governor's Heritage Award for best traditional artist in Vermont.

Maria Barton
Indian River, Michigan

Maria began hooking in 1992 and owns and operates Star Rug Company, a web-based rug hooking pattern business. She is best known for her primitive style and her whimsical primitive patterns.

Maria has written articles for both *Rug Hooking* magazine and *Wool Street Journal*. She was recognized in 2005 and 2006 by *Early American Life* magazine as one of the top 100 artisans in the country. Her rugs have been featured in magazines including *Early American Life*, *Celebrate*, and *Country Almanac*. Maria teaches at camps and workshops throughout the United States.

SHOWCASE OF

Original Designs

A work composed firsthand

Merriam Webster's Collegiate Dictionary, 11th edition

ORIGINAL

An original rug is designed and hooked from an original idea with original content and interpretation.

A Memory of the Baltic Sea

Hildegardt Sawyer had so many memories of her homeland in East Prussia, Germany, that she decided to hook some of them into this scene of the Baltic Coast as a way to help her both remember the pleasant parts of her past and put other memories to rest.

Hildegardt color planned the rug and used Cushing spot and dip dyes to create the shades from her memories. She used very little recycled wool, incorporating mostly new wool from Dorr and Woolrich. Hildegardt whipped the edges of the rug with a dark brown wool and hung the finished rug in her living room. Her favorite parts of the rug are the sky and the sea.

The wide intricate hooked frame was the most difficult part of the rug. She used colors from the image in the center of the rug, but she wanted to create a repetitive design that would be wildly different from the landscape scene at the rug's heart. "It was a boring task to hook the border," she said.

Hildegardt came to America when Eisenhower was president. She had lost her mother to multiple sclerosis and she lost her father, three brothers, and one sister during the war. She remembers running away from her hometown to escape the advancing Russian Army, being sworn into the German Army, and finally crossing the Moldau River at the end of the war to reach the safety of a camp for refugees.

"When I was hooking this rug, with every loop, the tragic past sank into the bottom of the sea," she said. "And I have found peace."

In the Judges' Words

- *Very interesting treatment for border.*
- *Exquisite detail.*
- *Breathtaking!*

HILDEGARDT SAWYER
BUNKER HILL, WEST VIRGINIA

When Hildegardt came to America in 1956 she was 25 and spoke only two phrases in English: "good night" and "good-bye." In 1973, she started a small framing business, which is where she met Joyce Schroeder, a rug hooker and customer who kept nudging Hildegardt to try rug hooking until she could no longer say no. Hildegardt has completed 11 rugs since 2001. Her inclusion in Celebration is her first award for one of her rugs.

A Memory of the Baltic Sea, 71" x 52", #3- and 4-cut wool on rug warp. Designed and hooked by Hildegardt M. Sawyer, Bunker Hill, West Virginia, 2010. PHOTO BY BILL BISHOP, IMPACT XPOSURES

Feather Hearth Rug

Feather Hearth Rug, 68" x 13", #3-, 6-, and 8-cut wool on monk's cloth. Designed and hooked by Kathleen Harwood, Montrose, Pennsylvania, 2010. PHOTO BY VAN ZANDERBERGEN PHOTOGRAPHY

Kathleen Harwood is inspired by historical American decorative arts, such as this classic feather quilting pattern. "I love the undulating, graceful character of the design," she said. "It struck me as perfect for a long, narrow hearth rug."

Kathleen started with a colorful but soft palette in the feather, which she thought would give her a softly toned rug—a color scheme that is in sharp contrast to Kathleen's more frequent and much bolder color selections. "But when I began considering background wool [for the center field], the coral called out to me," she said. "Then I was right back into my color comfort zone."

Kathleen frequently uses recycled wool in her projects, but she chose all new wool for *Feather.* Dozens of the colors were pulled from her own stash. The wool for the central vein of the feather was spot dyed by Vivily Powers. Vivily also dyed the cream and gray-green mottled wool that Kathleen used to outline the cream field around the feather.

The most difficult part of hooking this rug, Kathleen noted, was learning to adapt to changing ideas. "I thought each lobe of the feather would be a different color," she said. "As I began to hook, I found myself mixing the colors. That quickly became rewarding—and rather tedious—to hook."

Overall, Kathleen is thrilled with the finished rug. "I love the rug as a whole," she said. "It's all about the successful marriage of design and color and craftsmanship."

In the Judges' Words

- Nice workmanship.
- Many tiny bits of color in the feather make this piece effective and interesting.
- The hooked tongues look real.

KATHLEEN HARWOOD
MONTROSE, PENNSYLVANIA

Kathleen is president of her own company, Harwood Fine Arts, where she works as a consultant, appraiser, and dealer. She has been a fine art appraiser on Antiques Roadshow, a popular PBS television series, since its initial season in 1995. Kathleen learned to hook under the tutelage of Claire deRoos and Nancy MacLennan. She estimates she's hooked 40 pieces, with 15 of those being rugs. Feather is her second rug to appear in Celebration.

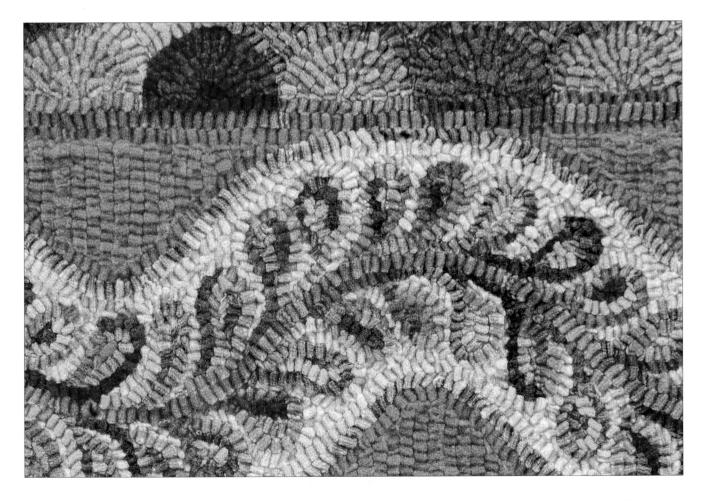

Fishing Day

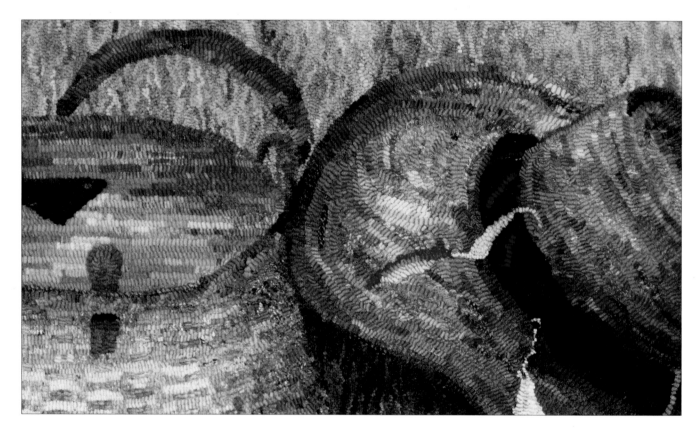

*F*ishing Day is the first rug in a new series that Capri Boyle Jones plans to dedicate to the men in her life. "It represents freshwater fishing, which all my guys enjoy," she said. "It also represents a fond memory of provision and enjoyment by my grandfathers."

Capri noted that the wools in the basket and the hat are a combination of dyed and as-is wool from her "stash in variety." "I dye practically every style and shelve the wool according to type so I can pull it for use as needed," she said. The background grass and sky wools are gradations dyed by Genevieve Patterson. Capri separated them into piles of light, medium, and dark "to utilize them in a painterly fashion."

To achieve the watercolor-like effect, Capri also used a wide variety of techniques and cuts. She hooked the background from several pounds of leftover #3-cut wool, with a handful of other cuts tossed in. The basket is a #5 cut with the lid and strap hooked in a #8. The hat and rod are predominately a #8 cut.

The most challenging part of creating her design was learning to hook what Capri calls "the naturals"—the wood, grass, leather, and sky—in a realistic manner. "I learned to see

mentally and visually the temperature of the neutral values of my wools," she said. "This created the impression of light while maintaining a close realistic interpretation of scene and memory."

To finish the rug, Capri whipped the edges to match the loop colors.

CAPRI BOYLE JONES
NAVARRE, FLORIDA

Capri started hooking rugs to cover the floors of her 50-plus-year-old home. Now she creates her own designs based on images that remind her of her family, both current and past.

In the 20 years that she has been rug hooking, Capri has finished more than 145 rugs, pillows, stools, and wearables. She is a McGown certified teacher who holds memberships in both the McGown Guild and ATHA. Fishing Day is her third rug to be featured in Celebration.

Fishing Day, 46" x 26", #3-, 5-, and 8-cut wool on linen. Designed and hooked by Capri Boyle Jones, Navarre, Florida, 2010.

In the Judges' Words

- *Exceptional artistry!*
- *Shading of hat and carry-on is great.*
- *Background is perfect.*

Forever Plaid

When Debbie Clement couldn't find the right rug for her dining room, she decided to hook one herself. She sent numerous pictures of the room and fabric samples to her teacher Sharon Saknit. "We decided to incorporate the colors and plaid of the curtains along with the fruit centerpiece and the blue and white floral China as the main design elements," Debbie said. "The rug was actually two rugs in one: a plaid rug and a fruit and floral rug."

To find just the right color matches for their plan, the two women spent several hours combing through Sharon's wool bins. Sharon dyed swatches for the fruit and Debbie dyed the gold center background using the casserole method. The plaid was five colors of wool straight off the bolt.

Debbie found the thick plaid border the most challenging part of this rug. "I tried three different methods of hooking plaid before finding the one that produced the most satisfying results," she said. "I spent 10 hours hand drawing the plaid lines on the rug warp to make sure every line was drawn perfectly straight. It would have been impossible to achieve a true plaid without this preparation."

Debbie also struggled with the monotone colors of the delft fruit. "Shading has always been a challenge for me as I'm not a natural artist," she said. Debbie turned to Sharon for guidance on making the fruit appear three-dimensional.

Debbie finished the rug by rolling the edge forward and whipstitching it with yarn.

In the Judges' Words

- *Flowers were shaded quite well.*
- *Lovely color plan.*
- *Fantastic plaid background.*

DEBBIE CLEMENT
CLOVIS, CALIFORNIA

Handcrafts have always been interesting to Debbie, but it was the idea of using recycled wool that really caught her imagination. In the past nine years, she has hooked 19 items, including rugs, pillows, chair pads, a purse, and other small pieces. She is a member of ATHA and several local organizations, and her work has won ribbons at the Fresno County Fair. Forever Plaid is her first rug to be entered in Celebration.

Forever Plaid, 26¹/₂" x 62¹/₂", #4- and 6-cut wool on rug warp.
Designed and hooked by Debbie Clement, Clovis, California, 2010. PHOTO BY BEN CLEMENT PHOTOGRAPHY

Free Spirits

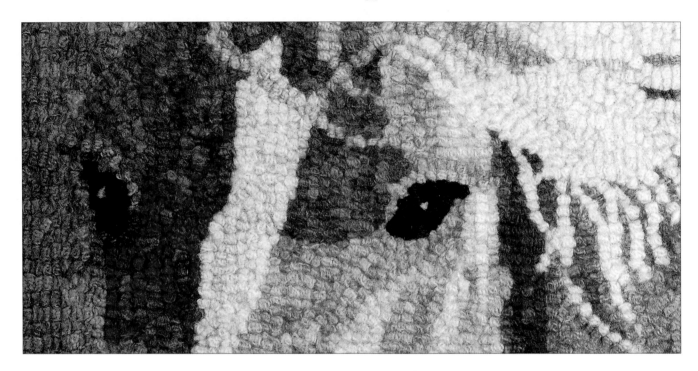

Mary Beth Westcott hooked what she considered to be the most difficult area of *Wild Spirits* first—the horses' faces. However, she soon found out that the legs of the horses were even more of a challenge.

"I wanted to name the rug 'Two Mares and Eight Dang Legs,'" she said. "It was such a challenge to sort the legs out in my mind—and while hooking. I pushed myself to finish one leg at a time to keep progressing."

Mary Beth combined her love of photography and rug hooking in the creation of this rug. With her camera, she captured an image of two Haflinger mares in action. "The photo also illustrated the personalities of the two horses," she said, "with the lead mare being very adventurous and the other more sophisticated and reserved."

Mary Beth used Photoshop to enlarge the photo, add a new background, and create a final visual aid from which to work. She dyed wools in progressive values of solid colors to duplicate the shading of the horses' coats, taking her freshly dyed wool out into the pasture to see how well her results matched the real animals. For the background colors she chose spot dyed wools by Karen Maddox.

During the rug hooking process, Mary Beth consulted with her teacher Judy Rippstein. "Under her watchful eye, I was able to accomplish so much more," she said. "She was always spot-on with her suggestions."

Mary Beth whipped the edges of the rug to match the background, sometimes using a different color for each of the three plies. She plans to hang the finished rug in the bunkhouse at her ranch.

In the Judges' Words

- *Can almost feel the speed and wind and hear the pounding hoofs.*
- *Impressive workmanship and exquisite shading.*
- *Well done!*

MARY BETH WESTCOTT
GONZALES, TEXAS

Mary Beth, owner of Wood N Wool, enjoys designing rugs because she sees it as a form of "make believe" that we all enjoyed in our childhood. She began hooking rugs after seeing a primitive hooked rug on eBay. In the past 10 years, Mary Beth has hooked about a dozen rugs and has half that many in various stages of completion. Free Spirits is her first rug to be included in Celebration.

Free Spirits, 21" x 32", #2- and 3-cut wool on rug warp.
Designed and hooked by Mary Beth Westcott, Gonzales, Texas, 2010. PHOTO BY BULL SAWNSON

Friends on the Rock

imone Vojvodin had punch hooked several rugs featuring single dogs and geometric or simple backgrounds. With this rug, she wanted to accomplish two goals: hook more than one dog and attempt a more realistic background.

She chose her sister's two dogs, Casey and Sophie, as her subjects and positioned them on their favorite rock. "I worked more toward capturing the feeling of the place than reproducing it," she said. She knew she had the design right when she emailed a pencil sketch to her sister and got a teary—but positive—response.

Simone did a lot of experimenting with colors. "I created a really interesting assortment of yarn by doing regular, spot, and dip dyeing," she said. "It was great fun to see what crazy wool was going to come out of my pot." She used monk's cloth for the backing and hooked it with heavy, rug-weight wool yarn.

Simone's favorite part of the rug is the little dog's face. "It was a joy hooking Sophie with her funny expressive look," she said.

One extremely challenging part of hooking this rug was duplicating the colors in the dogs' coats. Simone experimented with different dye combinations and layered in the colors as she was hooking in order to get more realistic results.

To finish the rug, Simone ran cording along the edge and whipped it with rug yarn. "I like that it allows for a rug to be hung with either the front or the back showing, as the back has its own special look," she said.

In the Judges' Words

- Lots of good detail.
- Captures the spirit of cherished pets.
- The dogs are terrific.

SIMONE VOJVODIN
PARKHILL, ONTARIO, CANADA

Simone found a copy of an old issue of Celebration at her local library and decided to try punch hooking. One of the dozen projects she's created over the last year is a life-sized Bernese Mountain dog that sits beside her couch and startles visitors who think the piece is real. Simone recently started her own pattern business, Red Maple Ruggery. Her inclusion in Celebration is her first award for her rugs.

Friends on the Rock, 3-ply rug wool on monk's cloth. Designed and hooked by Simone Vojvodin, Parkhill, Ontario, Canada, 2010.

Full Bloom

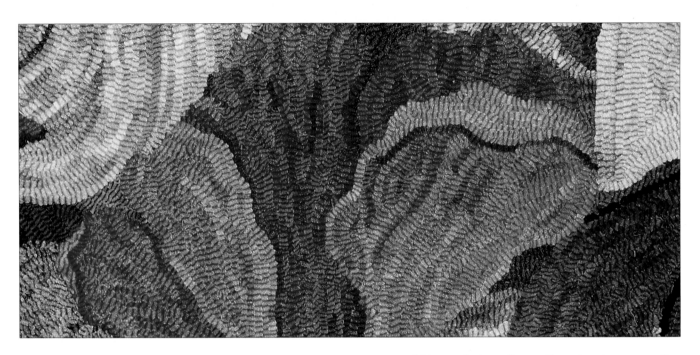

ngela Possak has always loved the flow and movement of flowers in full bloom. "At this point they are at their full color and glory," she said, "and a great joy to hook." She chose this particular perspective to show the viewer the ever-changing shapes and movements of the flowers' petals.

Angela color planned the rug based on real flowers, using walks through gardens and books to make the colors as accurate as possible. "Realism was part of my design strategy," she said. "I wanted the colors to be as natural as they could be when working with wool."

All of the wool in Angela's rug was dyed with either spot, dip, or casserole dyes over new Dorr wool. "The dip-dyed wool already has the color values in place," she said, "allowing me to create a flower from this one swatch."

Angela created movement and depth in her rug by allowing the flowers, petals, and leaves to overlap. She used different dye techniques and color values to emphasize their relative positions. "Also, outlining a flower allows the viewer to easily see a petal turning," she said.

The leaves, though mostly covered by the flowers, play an important part in Angela's composition. Their colors range from light to dark, providing a background for the brighter flowers.

For Angela, the most challenging part of this rug was the placement and balance of the flowers. "I had to walk away and leave it for a time," she said. "Then I came back to it with a fresh perspective."

In the Judges' Words

- *Lovely petal texture through directional color blending.*
- *Shading is different and interesting.*
- *Nicely hooked.*

ANGELA POSSAK
PEACHLAND, BRITISH COLUMBIA, CANADA

A string of great mentors, starting with Betty Wills of Calgary, helped Angela to hone her rug hooking skills. She hasn't kept track of the number of rugs she's hooked in the past 33 years, but she estimates the figure to be more than 100. A full-time artist who recently started a rug hooking business under her own name, Angela is a McGown certified teacher. Full Bloom is her first rug to be featured in Celebration.

Full Bloom, 46″ x 33″, *#6-cut wool on Scottish burlap.*
Designed and hooked by Angela Possak, Peachland, British Columbia, Canada, 2010. PHOTO BY FELIX POSSAK

Fungi I

Lyle Drier never really considered fungi to be a topic for a hooked rug design. But after a hike in Door County, Wisconsin, Lyle found some incredible fungi that were definitely rug worthy. "The variety of shapes, colors, and sizes was truly amazing," she said. "It is great fun and quite a challenge to hook Mother Nature."

Always one to give credit where credit is due, Lyle noted that Mother Nature, not Lyle herself, did the color planning. She used some of the textured wool as is, then spot dyed some of the greens. Anne Boissinot dyed the rest of the greens and the oranges.

Lyle's favorite fungus in the composition is the shelf fungus at the top of the rug. "Who would have thought that there was purple and lime green in a real life fungus?" she said. The most difficult aspect of the rug was hooking the orange fungus. "I had some difficulty getting the depth and shape of the fungus to show."

Because some of the blocks already had a white border, Lyle simply finished the piece with rug binding. The finished rug hangs in the front hallway of her home.

Although she has not yet designed a companion rug for *Fungi I*, Lyle does have plenty of photos to create another rug with more types of fungi. "Hence the name *Fungi I*," she said.

In the Judges' Words

- *Unique and well-executed subjects.*
- *I like the way some overlap their borders.*
- *Colors are interesting and subject matter original.*

LYLE DRIER
WAUKESHA, WISCONSIN

An article in Woman's Day *magazine featuring hooked rugs inspired Lyle to start making her own rugs for her antique-filled home. She hooked her first rug in 1972— a Texas star pattern—and has completed more than 140 pieces since. She likes to hook geometrics but loves the challenge of hooking something outside her comfort zone. Her work has won numerous ribbons at the Wisconsin State Fair.* Fungi I *is her seventh rug to be featured in* Celebration.

Fungi I, 17¹/₂″ x 28¹/₄″, #3-, 4-, and 5-cut wool on monk's cloth.
Designed and hooked by Lyle Drier, Waukesha, Wisconsin, 2009. PHOTO BY ANN RUDOLPH

Hunter

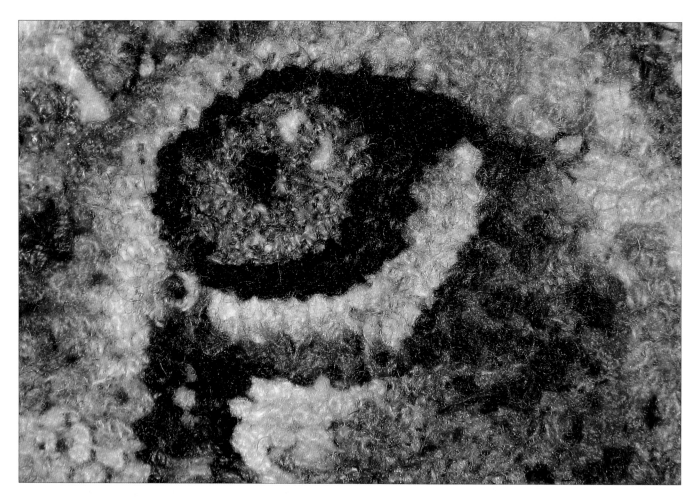

Judy Carter was inspired to design an image of a lion after a visit to a nearby zoo. "I was looking for a pattern I could use for a workshop," she said. "This beautiful lion caught my eye as the perfect subject."

Judy color planned the rug to focus all of the attention on the lion and his expression. "Most of the strips were textures I pulled from my stash to achieve the color variations and the look and feel of fur," she said. She penny dyed wool (pennies, ammonia, and sunshine) for the whiskers, under the eyes, and on the chin.

With any portrait, Judy starts with the eyes and facial features to set the tone of the rest of the composition. As she hooked the eyes, the lion quickly came to life. "I could feel him looking at me across the room whenever I came near the partially hooked rug," she said.

The most challenging part of completing the rug was deciding which wools to use after she had hooked the eyes, nose,

and mouth. She used more than 40 wools and found it hard to decide where to put them. "I organized my wool strips like a painter's palette and focused on the values of my wools," she said. "I followed my visual aid to achieve the contours of the face and the realistic look of fur."

Judy whipped the edges with wool yarn over cording and attached the outside edge of the rug tape as she whipstitched. The remaining edge of the tape was hand-sewn in place.

The finished rug hangs in the corner of her family room with three other big cat rugs.

In the Judges' Words

- *Beautifully shaded with a wide range of textures.*
- *The eyes are fabulous.*
- *Very realistic.*

Hunter, 20" x 20", #3- and 4-cut wool on rug warp. Designed and hooked by Judy Carter, Willow Street, Pennsylvania, 2010.

JUDY CARTER
WILLOW STREET, PENNSYLVANIA

Judy has hooked in everything from #2-cut wool to hand-ripped ¹/₂″ strips. She likes variety but has been focusing on close-up animal designs that use #3 and #4 cuts. Judy is an accredited McGown teacher, president of the McGown Northern Teachers Workshop, and secretary of the National Guild of McGown Hookrafters. She teaches classes and was the featured speaker at the 2010 Virginia Rug Fest. Hunter is her seventh rug to be featured in Celebration.

Island Sunrise

Sara Judith enjoys designing patterns that combine traditional rug hooking with punch hooking. "The creative possibilities within hooking are huge," she said. "*Island Sunrise* is a result of my exploration, combining the traditional detailed aspect of hooking with the explosion of color and texture available in punch hooking."

Sara color planned her rug based on views of several sunrises. "I love color," she said, "and this view of the sunrise looking back from Vancouver Island toward the mainland expresses the joy and hope of a new day."

To create a difference in texture between the landscape and the sunrise, Sara punch hooked the colored sky with many kinds of yarn, including wool, mohair, cotton and rayon chenille, silk, and boucles. The water and the silhouetted areas were hooked with mostly recycled wool.

Sara also employed directional hooking to separate the image into three distinct sections. The land and trees in the foreground were hooked vertically, the water and the mountains were hooked horizontally, and the sky was hooked in soft waves of undulating color.

The vividly colored sky is Sara's favorite part of the finished hooking. "I learned that a sunrise (or sunset) is a very forgiving sky to hook as there really isn't any error," she said. "The colors are glorious and you can adapt and change them at will."

Sara finished the rug by turning a hem to the back. The rug is mounted with Velcro to hang above a sideboard and below windows in her dining room.

In the Judges' Words

- *Pleasing use of color in lovely hues of sky and water.*
- *Beautifully done silhouettes against a richly colored background.*
- *Terrific. Very well done.*

SARA JUDITH
NELSON, BRITISH COLUMBIA, CANADA

Sara has attended many rug hooking workshops and schools over the past seven years but feels she learns the most by developing her sense of color, design, and technique on her own. A pharmacist by trade, she received her McGown certification and Amy Oxford punch needle instructor certification in 2009. She also enjoys weaving and spinning and recently learned to knit. Island Sunrise is her third rug to be featured in Celebration.

Island Sunrise, 68" x 14", #8-cut wool and various yarns on monk's cloth. Designed and hooked by Sara Judith, Nelson, British Columbia, Canada, 2010. PHOTO BY HEATHER GOLDSWORTHY

Jazz for the Night Owls

All of the action in Susan Cunningham's rug started with her husband's glance at a folk art birdhouse in Susan's home office. That alligator playing a saxophone, which is also the three-foot-tall birdhouse, became the focal point of the rug.

"Together we amplified the concept to include three animals playing musical instruments," she said. "Then came the full moon and owls in spooky trees." As she drew the design, she fleshed it out even more with animals by a fire, a baby raccoon, a frog, a turtle. . . "I wanted to put in a small squirrel someplace, but Dave said enough already."

Susan faced several challenges in hooking this rug. When she cut the off-white wool that she had dyed as swatches for the blue sky, she found that the core of the wool was still whitish. "I spent a lot of time nit-picking the tiny, errant tufts of white off the edges of the strips," she said.

The hills were also a challenge. The more she hooked, the more the previous areas seemed to stand out. Susan's remedy—dyeing more spot dyes—resulted in a number of different colors in the hills, but she felt they blended together well.

Susan eventually gave up her wish for a red border. She tried dark red for the lettering instead but found that the words got lost when she viewed the rug from a distance. "I did allow myself two rows of dark red around the border and whipped the edge with a red yarn," she said.

In the Judges' Words

- *Thoughtful use of color and attention to detail contribute to a great piece.*
- *Brightly colored animals add to the whimsy.*
- *Well done.*

SUSAN CUNNINGHAM
LARAMIE, WYOMING

Susan finds that the same characteristics that make her a successful computer software designer—precision placement of motifs and colors, attention to detail, and perseverance—carry over into rug hooking. She has completed 11 rugs since 2004, with her husband, Dave, being her most valued critic. Her rugs have been featured in Wren, *Wyoming's statewide rural electric co-op news magazine.* Jazz for the Night Owls *is her fourth rug to be featured in* Celebration.

Jazz for the Night Owls, 53" x 43", #3- and 4-cut wool on linen.
Designed and hooked by Susan M. Cunningham, Laramie, Wyoming, 2010. PHOTO BY LARAMIE DIGITAL PHOTO CENTER

Lady Sunset

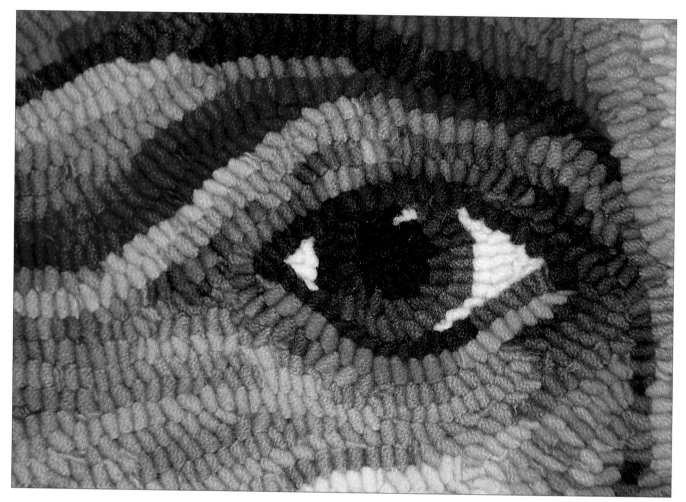

April DeConick drew this design for the Kirby Hooking Circle's 2010 Celestial Challenge. "I knew I wanted to hook a sun with a face," she said. "My inspiration came from ancient artisans and how they depicted feelings of dread and awe in their portrayals of ancient gods and angels."

April color planned the rug, dyeing each of the colors in an 8-value swatch in a method she created and named Palette Dyeing. "All seven colors in the sun were created by mixing yellow with other colors on the color wheel, so the colors are related to each other on the most basic level," she said. "This creates a very harmonious and striking effect." The wool strips for the sun and the rays were dyed over white wool; the background is textured wool over dyed with brown.

To make the sun stand out from the background, April hooked the brown background strips with the pebble stitch. The sun, which April hooked and rehooked several times, is done in three different methods: directional hooking for the center, a perpendicular single row circle to separate the center from the rays, and a random placement of loops for the rays.

April's favorite part of the finished rug is the eyes. "They were the first thing I hooked," she said. "Once I sat back and gazed at her, I had a real sense that she was coming to life."

April finished the rug using a Canadian show-binding technique. She bound strips of the background wool around the edge, turned it under, and hand-tacked it to the back.

In the Judges' Words

- *Imaginative composition.*
- *Extremely well done.*
- *Artistry and color play good.*

Lady Sunset, 24" x 24",
#6 hand-dyed wool on linen.
Designed and hooked by April
D. DeConick, Houston,
Texas, 2010.

APRIL DeCONICK
HOUSTON, TEXAS

April, a religious studies professor, knew that rug hooking was "it" when she
saw a demonstration at the Waterloo Historical Farm in Michigan, but she
admits having to work at the basics. "I was not a natural," she said. "I struggled to pull decent loops." Between 1995 and today—with time off to raise her
son—April has hooked 30 rugs and started an Internet business, Red Jack
Rugs. Lady Sunset is her second rug to be featured in Celebration.

Magic Carpet Runner

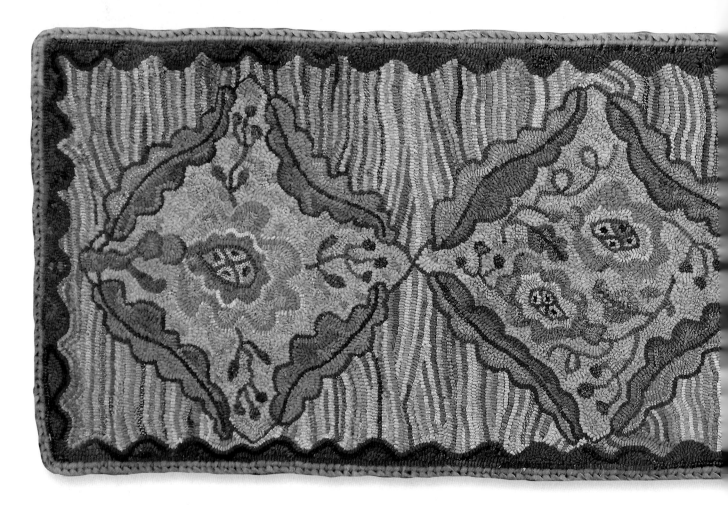

Karen Kahle designed this primitive rug to compete with more realistic and busy rugs. "Primitive designs are often understated and so simple in their overall effect that it is difficult to compete with other rugs," she said. "I thought this primitive had enough complexity to stand out."

Karen loves all things with ripples, and incorporating a rippled effect into her design was a top priority. Gathering inspiration from antique rugs, Karen planned the colors to duplicate the faded look of an older rug. The red outline was an element directly pulled from other vintage rugs.

Karen always uses wool from her stash, usually dyeing a few key colors to add variety. She over dyed as is, marbleized, textured, and solid wools to get the colors she needed. "I love the way special textures punctuate the hand-dyed solid colors."

Karen's favorite part of the rug is the interplay of soft versus sharp edges. The flowers, leaves, and tendrils are hooked in soft focus, which contrast sharply with the red scalloped border

and the lines of the background. Her biggest challenge was choosing the right red. "I didn't want the red to glow or to make the aqua glow, so the red had to be toned down," she said. "I chose several dusty, warm reds, using all of them for variation."

As with all of Karen's rugs, she finished the runner with a crocheted edge. She uses long strips of wool in a #7- or 8-cut and single crochets them over the double-folded foundation fabric.

In the Judges' Words

- *Hit or miss background is well done.*
- *Thoughtfully composed design.*
- *Overall mood and simplicity achieved through great attention to detail.*

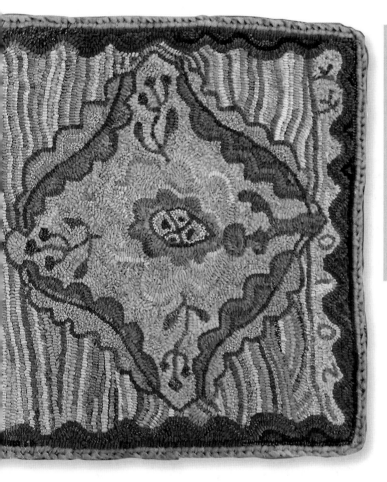

KAREN KAHLE
EUGENE, OREGON

After Karen saw an article on rug hooking with naturally dyed wools in American Life magazine, she started collecting wool in anticipation of the day when she would start to hook her own rugs. In the past 14 years, she has hooked 140 rugs, bags, pillows, and wall hangings. Karen owns Primitive Spirit, through which she sells patterns, videos, and dye books. Magic Carpet Runner is her first rug to be featured in Celebration.

Magic Carpet Runner, 64" x 24", #6-, 7-, and 8-cut wool on linen. Designed and hooked by Karen Kahle, Eugene, Oregon, 2010.

Majestic Moose

Rochelle Stibb's husband's love of North American wildlife inspired her to design this image of a moose in the wild. "He enjoys wild animals like bear, elk, and deer," she said. "I wanted to hook a rug that he would like to have around the house."

Rochelle color planned her rug in a rather unconventional method. With the help of her friend Jeannine Paul, she bought a stack of brown wool in a wide range of hues and values. With those wools, she hooked the moose. When the moose was completely hooked, she bought the wool for the mountains and hooked them. She repeated the same steps with the lake, the grass, the foreground, the sky, and the border. "I found it easier to concentrate on one area at a time," she said.

Most of the wool used in the rug was over dyed, except the sky. Rochelle and Jeannine dip dyed the colors for the sky in three sections: peach to light peach, purple to periwinkle blue,

and light peach to light purple. "I felt we needed to dye that third piece of wool for the sky to make the transition more gradual," she said.

Rochelle needed two years to finish her rug but was surprised by "what really can be accomplished in all those '15 minutes here, 20 minutes there,'" she said. She was also pleased and amazed that her concept of the rug didn't change over those two years. "The final rug looks exactly as I envisioned it would look two years earlier."

In the Judges' Words

- *Distance is well portrayed in grassy foreground against distant landscape.*
- *Handsome shading of the animal.*
- *A lot of detail for a #8 cut.*
- *Spectacular colors!*

ROCHELLE STIBB
BEAVER DAM, WISCONSIN

Rochelle, a graphic artist, is an award-winning quilter who is new to rug hooking. She works her rug hooking time around a schedule that includes a full-time job and caring for young children. She shies away from primitive rug hooking patterns; instead she enjoys the challenge of hooking shaded, realistic designs with #8-cut wool. Majestic Moose *is her fourth rug, and her inclusion in* Celebration *is her first award for her rug hooking. Rochelle's website is www.RochelleStibb.com.*

Majestic Moose, 53¹/₂″ x 38″, #8-cut recycled and new wool on linen.
Designed and hooked by Rochelle Stibb, Beaver Dam, Wisconsin, 2010.

Mighty Moose

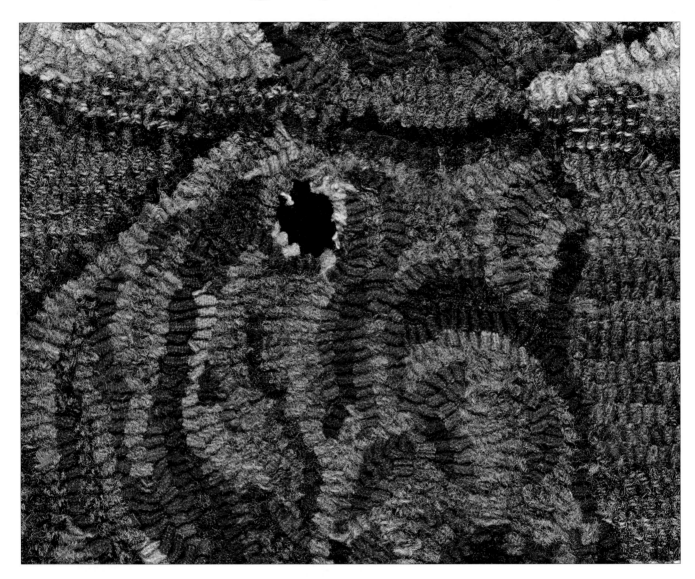

Fritz Mitnick hooked this rug as a reminder of spending one of the shortest days of the year—Christmas—in Alaska with her family. She included the two things that impressed her the most about the trip: the colors and the moose. "The mountains blocked the sun," she said, "so what little daylight we had was always a purpley pink that reflected off the snow . . . The moose were huge, but when they were standing still we often didn't notice their presence until we were too close."

Fritz color planned the background using reference photos of moose and her memories of the purple-tinged sky and countryside. "For the background, I used 10 different wools, mostly textures over dyed with a plum formula," she said. Everything else was hooked from odd bits of new wool that she had on hand.

Designing the moose proved to be the biggest challenge. "I had several photos, but nothing was quite right. And I never got the hooves right, so I buried them in snow."

Fritz's favorite part of the rug is the snow. "It makes me recall the colors that amazed me in Alaska."

Fritz finished the rug by rolling the excess linen to the front and overcasting with 100% wool yarn. She rotates the rugs in her home on a seasonal basis. *Mighty Moose* is the winter rug. It hangs from an antique butcher paper dispenser in the front hall.

FRITZ MITNICK
PITTSBURGH, PENNSYLVANIA

Fritz caught "rug hooking-itis" when she won a Charlotte Price rug at the 1997 Pittsburgh Rug Hooking Guild's biennial show. Every Monday after that, she left work to spend her lunch hour learning to rug hook with the local guild members. Fritz has hooked 40 large rugs and 100 smaller pieces. She is a McGown accredited teacher and regularly donates rugs to charity auctions. Mighty Moose is her third rug to be featured in Celebration.

Mighty Moose, 18" x 42", #7-cut wool on linen. Designed and hooked by Fritz Mitnick, Pittsburgh, Pennsylvania, 2010.

PHOTO BY ALAN J. KING

My African Ladies

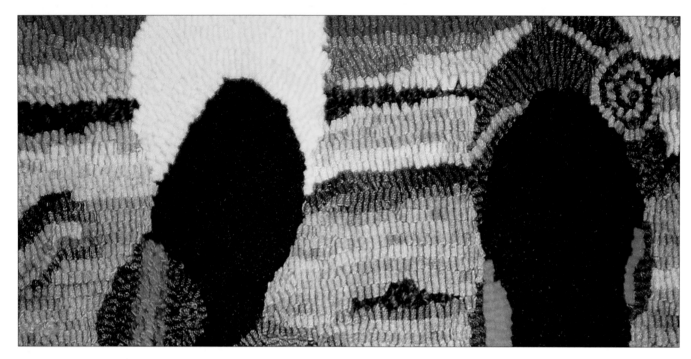

Every time Frances Rendon looks at this rug, she remembers the two mission trips she took to Kenya and Tanzania. "These women represent the ladies I met," she said. "During my mission trips, each one made me a member of her family." The absence of faces on the women is central to Frances' design. "It allows me to place the many ladies I've met and seen into the rug," she said, "without picking only four."

Frances color planned the rug with Nancy Miller Quigley, who helped her pick out the Cushing dyes that made her rug come to life. Frances dyed the wool a half-yard at a time, using the open pot method. The brown wool in the background is a textured wool used as is.

Frances noted that the most difficult part of this rug was dyeing the wool for the blue dress of the second lady from the left. The women from Benin, Kenya, are known for their beau-

tifully dyed fabric, which is tied with grass before the dyeing process begins. To make an authentic-looking garment, Frances dyed several different values of the same color and hooked them in vertical lines.

Frances finished the rug in three weeks and whipped the edges with hand-dyed wool yarn. The rug hangs on her living room wall surrounded by photographs of her trips.

"I think I was able to hook this rug so fast because its subject is so close to my heart," she said. "As I hooked, memories flowed and made me smile."

FRANCES RENDON
PLACERVILLE, CALIFORNIA

Frances, a retired U.S. Air Force master sergeant, has hooked 39 rugs, purses, and totes in the past 11 years. She tries to hook each day, even if it's only one strip. Frances is a member of the McGown guild, Region 12 of ATHA, and the Apple Hill Ruggers, and is working on her McGown certification. She has won numerous awards at county fairs. My African Ladies is her second rug to be featured in Celebration.

In the Judges' Words

- *Impressive workmanship and creativity.*
- *Bright colors against a softer tone landscape suggest culture being portrayed.*
- *Design elements breaking the border line add interest.*

My African Ladies, 24¹/2″ x 33″, #5-cut new wool on linen.
Designed and hooked by Frances Rendon, Placerville, California, 2010. PHOTO BY STEPHEN METCALF

My Lissa

Cheryl Halliday decided to design a rug based on her sheltie, Melissa, for a class with Jon Ciemiewicz at the Highlands School of Rug Hooking. She completed the face with Jon's help then worked on the rest of the rug with a local teacher, Vicki Calu.

Cheryl likes the combination of blue and green together and chose those colors for the fictitious quilt for Lissa to sit on. She hooked the rest of the rug to mimic a hardwood floor because she felt the colors and flatness balanced the tans and rusts in the dog's curly coat.

The only dyeing Cheryl did was a light over dye of navy to tie the colors of the quilt together. The remainder of the wool is new and recycled as-is wool. She picked a taupe and brown plaid for the dog's lighter fur and a Black Watch plaid, which was mostly navy and dark green, for the darker shades.

Hooking the quilt was quite a challenge. Because the fabric is folded under Lissa's body, Cheryl needed to change the direction of the quilt design in several areas. Cheryl finished the rug with strips of wool stitched around cording. The cording was hand-sewn to the edge of the rug to continue the color plan to the edge, then stitched to the back with rug tape.

Sadly, Lissa became ill and died before Cheryl finished the rug. "I entered the rug in *Celebration* because I promised her I would finish it and make it a winner just like her," Cheryl said.

In the Judges' Words

- *Quilt and wood floor add depth.*
- *Interesting perspective looking down on the dog.*
- *Love the asymmetry in this rug.*

CHERYL HALLIDAY
HATBORO, PENNSYLVANIA

Cheryl has been doing a variety of fiber arts for most of her life but recently turned to rug hooking at the urging of a close friend. In the past five years, she has completed seven rugs, a handbag, and a large tote bag. She is a member of the McGown guild, ATHA, the Old Barn Rug Hooking Guild, and the Hunterdon County Rug Artisans Guild. My Lissa is her first rug to appear in Celebration.

My Lissa, 36″ x 24″, #3-, 4-, and 5-cut wool on linen.
Designed and hooked by Cheryl Halliday, Hatboro, Pennsylvania, 2009. PHOTO BY BILL BISHOP, IMPACT XPOSURES

Peace

Grace Collette's sons love to see deer in the wild, so Grace set out to capture that feeling of awe with an atmosphere of peace and beauty. "After completing two commercial patterns, I read many books on composition and design," she said. "I'm enjoying this opportunity to explore my own creativity."

Grace color planned the rug, which she describes as the easy part. "I wanted warm colors for the focal point and the complementary color (purple) with some green for a limited color palette," she explained. She used dip dyes, spot dyes, and swatches over plaids, used clothing, and new wool to create the colors.

Peace is Grace's first attempt at designing a rug, which she noted as the most challenging part of this project. "I worked on one element at a time, with extensive research in rug hooking magazines and art books," she said. "As ardent hunters, my sons were a wonderful resource. It was a real family project."

Her extensive research paid off, because Grace is especially proud of her depiction of the deer's muscular definition. The pairing of lighter and darker wool colors in flowing lines emphasized the strong and beautiful nature of the animal.

Grace outlined the main images within the rug, including the deer, the trees, the cattails, the moon, and the owl. The outlines—combined with directional hooking—help the viewer's eye to focus on the most important parts of the rug.

Grace whipped the edge with needlepoint yarn. The finished rug hangs in the living room of her home.

In the Judges' Words

- *Impressive use of highlight.*
- *Well done.*
- *Sky and water really make it come alive.*

GRACE COLLETTE
RAYMOND, NEW HAMPSHIRE

Grace, an accountant, town treasurer, and professor, counts herself fortunate to have been able to take lessons from Ruth Hall at the local YWCA. She started hooking rugs about 40 years ago, but she only counts five of those years as active since working two jobs left her very little time to practice her art. Grace's work has won special awards and blue ribbons at area fairs. Peace is her first rug to be featured in Celebration.

Peace, 2′ x 3′, #3-cut wool on linen. Designed and hooked by Grace Collette, Raymond, New Hampshire, 2010.

Phoenix Rising

Wayne Bressler chose this sketch for *Phoenix Rising* from several abstract drawings because of its interesting, silhouetted shape. "I like how some shapes touch just at the ends and others stand alone, creating positive and negative spaces that create a flowing effect."

After Wayne finalized the sketch he used colored pencils to make his initial color plan. "I gradated some of my shapes, creating a visual movement that I really liked," Wayne said. "Now my challenge was to incorporate this effect into my rug."

Wayne experimented with dyeing techniques. He cut lengths of yarn to the same size, bundled them together, then hand dipped a portion of the lengths in one color. After rinsing the yarn, he dyed the other portion in another color, overlapping some of the previous color to achieve a gradating effect. "It did seem very hit or miss at first," he said, "but the more I dyed, the better I got at this process."

Eventually satisfied with his technique, Wayne dyed all the colors for this project. He dip dyed wool to achieve graduated colors and created solid colors using the immersion method.

Wayne uses a Craftsman's rug punch needle to hook his designs. After completing several rugs, he has decided he likes the short loops of a #9 or #10 setting.

To finish the rug, Wayne corded the edge then whipstitched it, creating a modern, silhouetted shape. The rug covers the back of a couch in his studio and will remain there on display until Wayne finishes his next rug.

In the Judges' Words

- *Excellent finishing work.*
- *Well-balanced color plan of vivid hues and contrast.*
- *Fascinating idea.*

WAYNE BRESSLER
NEW YORK, NEW YORK

As Wayne prepared his portfolio for entrance into art school, he included a punch needle hand-hooked rug with a planetary theme. Many years later he rediscovered rug hooking after remembering that punch tool he used to make his first rug. Now a graphic designer at Conde Nast Traveler magazine, Wayne has hooked 13 rugs and has several ideas and sketches waiting to be started. Phoenix Rising is his fourth rug to be chosen as a Celebration finalist.

Phoenix Rising, 25″ x 58″, *rug wool on monk's cloth. Designed and hooked by Wayne Bressler, New York, New York, 2010.*

ORIGINAL DESIGNS

Slumber

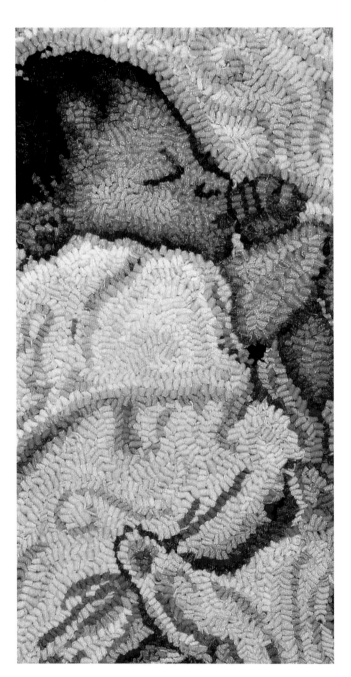

Rachelle LeBlanc designed *Slumber* to commemorate the day her daughter Emmanuelle came home from the hospital. "After Emmanuelle was born, I had severe post-partum depression and I don't remember much of her first year," Rachelle said. "With this rug, which inspired a series, I am trying to recapture moments that I don't remember, or simply forgot."

Rachelle used a photograph of Emmanuelle wrapped in a baby blanket to create the design for her rug. "I had composed the picture so I could paint her one day," she said. Rachelle eliminated the elements of the photo that weren't essential—"like the cute bunnies in the background"—concentrating on what she wanted to convey in this piece of art.

To achieve the lifelike colors of the baby's skin, Rachelle used a dyeing technique she developed and calls "underpainting." "Sometimes a painter will use a thin film of oil paint to create a base coat that will reflect in the next layer of paint. That's how I dye my wool," she said. Rachelle first dyed the wool in a baby pink or baby blue and then dyed the skin tones. "Dyeing this way gives the colors more depth."

Rachelle finished the rug with a chain stitch, which is a technique she developed as an alternative to whipstitching rugs that would be hung on museum and gallery walls.

A self-taught artist, Rachelle hooks with a latch hook and no frame. Her favorite part of this rug is its simplicity and delicacy. "It reminds me that anything is possible," she said.

In the Judges' Words

- *Subtle curves in the background add mood to lovely shaded child.*
- *Feet hooked into the border is unexpected and fun.*
- *Evokes emotion well.*

RACHELLE LEBLANC
ST. ALBERT, ALBERTA, CANADA

A trip to the Shelburne Museum in Vermont inspired Rachelle to learn rug hooking. She has finished 58 rugs since 2003, and the art has become a way for her to relieve stress and express her creativity. Her favorite topics to hook are images of people and she prefers using wide-cut strips of wool. Rachelle exhibits her work in area museums and is a member of the Alberta Craft Council. Slumber is her first rug to be featured in Celebration.

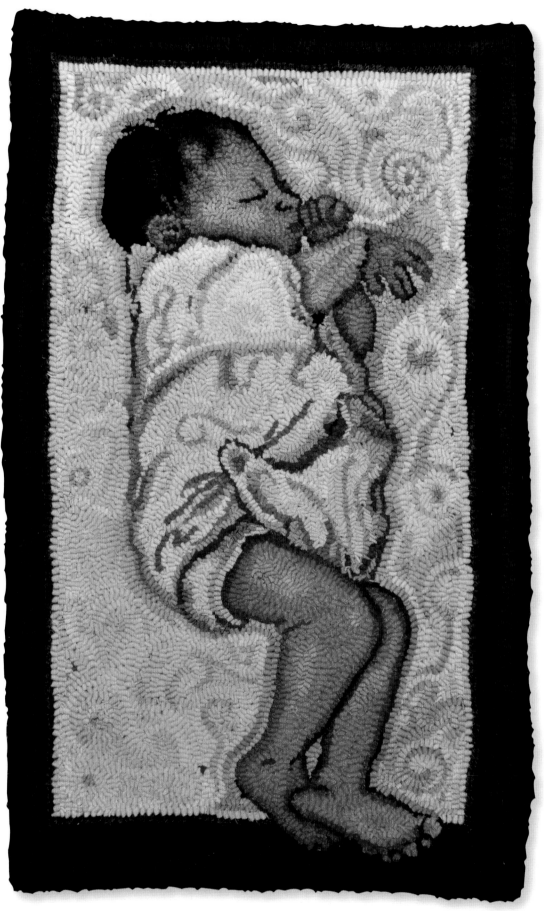

Slumber, 28" x 18", #4-, 6-, and 8-cut wool and cashmere on linen.
Designed and hooked by Rachelle LeBlanc, St. Albert, Alberta, Canada, 2010.

Snowmen Fall from Heaven Unassembled

Joyce Krueger saw the saying "Snowmen fall from heaven unassembled" on her church's bulletin board and knew an image built around those words would make a great rug—no matter how long it took. "From finding the saying, thinking about the rug, drawing. . . It was probably five years," she said. "The actual hooking took six months."

Joyce gathered ideas for her rug into a folder. Pris Butler helped her to put all her thoughts together on paper at the Sauder Village Rug Hooking Retreat. Joyce dyed wools from her stockpile using the open pan method and swatch dyeing. Diane Stoffel dyed the wool for the sky with the salt shaker method.

To add interest and texture to the rug, Joyce employed several techniques. She created the illusion of snow piled on the trees by hooking white commercial yarn and wool strips slightly higher than the green wool; she used her handspun wool to create the fur of the snow people's coats; and she sculpted some of the tassels on the hats. Swirls in the sky that drop onto the hill give the feeling of falling snow.

Joyce noted that the most difficult areas to hook were the snow-covered hills. "I took them out several times," she said. "Finally I used the same colors for both hills, and it worked."

Joyce finished the rug with white binding stitched behind the last row of loops and folded to the back. The rug is displayed in her front hall or in her studio, depending on the weather.

In the Judges' Words

- *Cute idea.*
- *Beautifully executed!*
- *Artist did a nice job making the snowmen stand out against the white background.*

SNOWMEN FALL FROM

HEAVEN UNASSEMBLED

JOYCE KRUEGER
WAUKESHA, WISCONSIN

Joyce describes her feelings toward rug hooking as "love at first loop." She learned to hook rugs in 1976, during a time when she was trying out all sorts of arts and crafts. These days she enjoys working on all types of rug hooking and notes that her favorite style is whatever she has on her frame at that point in time. Joyce has completed 150 pieces and is an accredited McGown teacher. Snowmen Fall from Heaven Unassembled is her second rug to be featured in Celebration.

Snowmen Fall from Heaven Unassembled, 29¹/₂" x 31¹/₂", #3- to 6-cut wool and wool yarn on monk's cloth. Designed and hooked by Joyce Krueger, Waukesha, Wisconsin, 2009. PHOTO BY MICHELLE AT ART'S CAMERA

The Happy Hoofer

Every time she looks at this rug, Linda Green is reminded of a recent vacation to Colorado. "This cow stayed in the middle of the road and didn't move," she said. "We had to go around her!"

Linda had plenty of time to take a picture of the stubborn bovine and knew the image would make a good memory rug. Sally Kallin, her teacher at the 2008 Ohio Rug Camp, color planned the rug and dyed new and recycled wool to match the photo.

The most challenging part of this rug was hooking the hills and the grasses. "I wanted to get enough detail in the hills so you could see the trees and the bushes, but not take away from the cow," she said. She hooked the grasses with three different golds and used a Fibonacci sequence to place the colors.

Linda receives many compliments on the accurate coloring of the road. To achieve the color play she wanted, Linda chose an as-is plaid wool with alternating gray and gray-blue stripes on a cream-white background.

Her favorite part of the rug is the cow. Linda worked hard to capture the cow's as-if-I-care attitude, and she is pleased with the results. "I love her face," she said. "Sally did a great job helping me to get the right look!"

To finish the rug, Linda rolled linen over cording and whipped the edge with double strands of black wool yarn. The rug hangs in her home's great room. "Rugs that are personal are the most fun to hook," she said.

In the Judges' Words

- *Very effective use of textures.*
- *Looks like a scene you see driving down a country road.*

LINDA GREEN
BEAVERCREEK, OHIO

Linda, a member of the Miami Valley ATHA guild, works at Wright-Patterson Air Force Base. She took her first rug hooking class with a friend through a local quilting and needlework store, then recruited two more friends. The four still hook once a month with seven other crafters.
Linda prefers primitive cuts and the look of antique rugs. The Happy Hoofer has been exhibited at Sauder Village, the Ohio Rug Camp, and the Beavercreek Rug Hooking Workshop.

The Happy Hoofer, 53″ x 36″, #8-cut wool on linen. Designed and hooked by Linda Green, Beavercreek, Ohio, 2010.

Winter Hunt

The dog in Mary McGrath's rug is her Vizsla, a Hungarian sporting dog. She designed the rug based on a photograph taken by her husband while they were out for a walk on a snowy winter morning.

Mary altered the photograph slightly by changing the object of the dog's attention. Instead of the brown chipmunk that blended into the winter grasses, Mary decided to hook a pheasant. "The bird is a fun surprise in the rug, and the red brings the viewer's eye to it after they first see the dog," she said.

Mary found the dog the most difficult part of the rug to design and hook, but she is especially proud of the way the muscle tone and shading worked on the dog's hindquarters. "That area turned out very believable and true to the original picture," she said. The snow—"because snow isn't white"— and the dog's shadow were two other challenging areas to hook.

Mary designed this rug to be auctioned off when her local Vizsla Club hosted the 50th anniversary of their national events in 2010. Unfortunately, Mother Nature had other plans. Mary was working on the sky when a tornado hit her home. She escaped safely to the basement, but her rug suffered multiple cuts to the backing from flying glass and debris. Instead of donating the finished rug, Mary decided to keep it. *Winter Hunt*, with its patches on the torn backing, is now displayed in the family room of her home.

In the Judges' Words

- *Shadow of the central figure reflected in the snow is effective.*
- *Well shaded throughout.*
- *Captures the intensity of a hunting dog on point.*

MARY MCGRATH
EAGLE, WISCONSIN

Mary started hooking rugs about eight years ago after she convinced herself that she really did need to start another hobby. Part of the deal was a personal rule that she would never start a new rug until the current rug was finished. So far, that rule has helped her to finish 11 rugs. She is a member of ATHA, and Winter Hunt is her first rug to be featured in Celebration.

Winter Hunt, 35″ x 18″, #3- and 4-cut wool on monk's cloth.
Designed and hooked by Mary McGrath, Eagle, Wisconsin, 2010. PHOTO BY MICHELLE AT ART'S CAMERAS

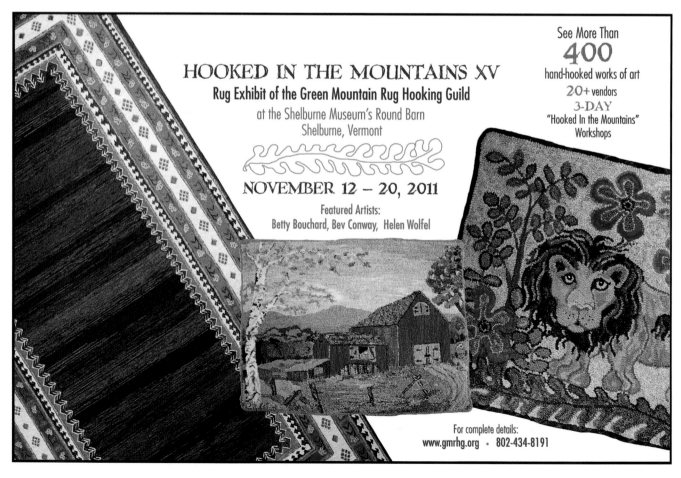

SHOWCASE OF
Commercial Designs

COMMERCIAL

A rug hooked from or substantially based on an existing commercially produced pattern.

Chi Chi

When Jeanne Benjamin started hooking *Chi Chi*, she didn't expect to find extraterrestrial beings in an Oriental rug pattern. "I began in the middle of the rug with what I called the 'aliens,' as they looked like motifs from early computer games," she said.

While they were fun to hook at first, Jeanne quickly found *Chi Chi's* aliens to be one of the most challenging aspects of the rug. "I set up a repeating pattern for them, but I never really stayed with it," she said. "They were fussy to do, so I would only hook two or three at a time before moving on to another section."

Jeanne color planned the rug, using wool that she had previously dyed from her own formulas. She didn't have a good color photograph of the finished piece to work from, but she did have an excellent mental picture of what she wanted. All of the strips she chose were cut from 100% over-dyed wool—

some of it new and some recycled. "I just pulled from my considerable stash until I was happy with the combination," she said.

Jeanne corded and whipped the edges with a dark red yarn, then added commercial fringe. While she can't point to a specific element as her favorite part of the rug, she is pleased with how the colors and patterns work together to deliver an authentic Oriental look. *Chi Chi* is currently waiting its turn to be displayed among the dozens of other rugs in Jeanne's rug hooking studio.

In the Judges' Words

- *Beautiful traditional colors.*
- *Well color planned.*
- *Excellent technique.*

JEANNE BENJAMIN
BROOKFIELD, MASSACHUSETTS

Jeanne has completed more than 250 hand-hooked rugs and small pieces in the past 40 years. She is a certified McGown instructor, teaching classes across the United States and in her own rug studio. She also runs a dyed wool business and owns New Earth Designs. Her days away from rug hooking are few and far between, but Jeanne wouldn't have it any other way. Chi Chi is her third rug to be featured in Celebration.

Chi Chi, 30" x 48", #4-cut hand-dyed wool on monk's cloth.
Designed by New Earth Designs; hooked by Jeanne Benjamin, Brookfield, Massachusetts, 2010. PHOTO BY JEREMIAH BENJAMIN

Girl in a Straw Hat

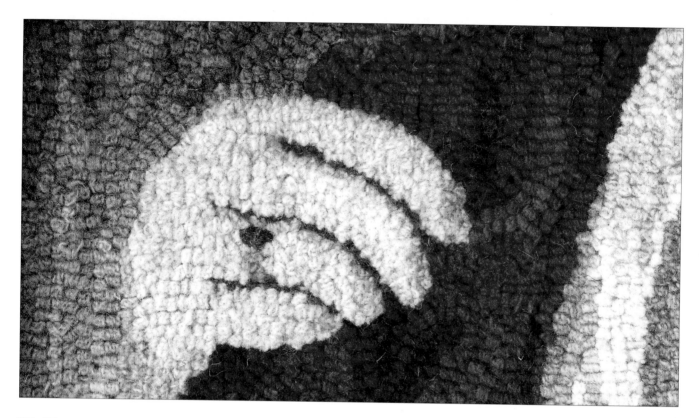

Karen Maddox was looking for a challenge when she chose to hook *Girl in a Straw Hat*. And she found one. Based on an 1884 painting by Pierre-Auguste Renoir called *Young Girl with Long Hair* or *Young Girl in a Straw Hat*, this pattern by Joan Moshimer features row after row of intricate shading. Karen color planned the rug using a photo of the artist's painting as reference. Her dye techniques included casserole, dip, and spot dyes over new wool.

Karen identified the girl's long, flowing hair as her favorite part of the rug to hook. "There was so much of it," she said, "and I tried to use as many different hues as I could and still have it read as 'red' hair."

The blue background, though it appeared easy to hook, was actually one of the more difficult areas. "I didn't want a solid background, so I interspersed a red with the mottled blue," she said. The most difficult area, Karen noted, was the shading in

the girl's face, especially around the nose and mouth. Her solution there was to hook that spot several times until it finally looked right.

Karen opted to frame the completed rug as a wall hanging instead of finishing it traditionally. She finds the end result stunning. "I have always enjoyed impressionist art, especially Renoir's work," she said. "I knew it would be a challenge to hook."

In the Judges' Words

- *Well-chosen colors enhance depth and contrast.*
- *The details in this rug are terrific.*

KAREN MADDOX
KERRVILLE, TEXAS

Curiosity got the best of Karen about 12 years ago as she passed by a class being taught by Jane Olson. She stopped in to see what the students were working on and ended up becoming an avid rug hooker. A McGown certified teacher, Karen has hooked 32 rugs and wall hangings and enjoys the challenges presented by pictorials hooked in narrow cuts. Girl is her sixth rug to be included in Celebration.

Girl in a Straw Hat, 16" x 18", #3- and 4-cut wool on burlap.
Designed by Joan Moshimer; hooked by Karen Maddox, Kerrville, Texas, 2009.

Hooking for Habitat Cube

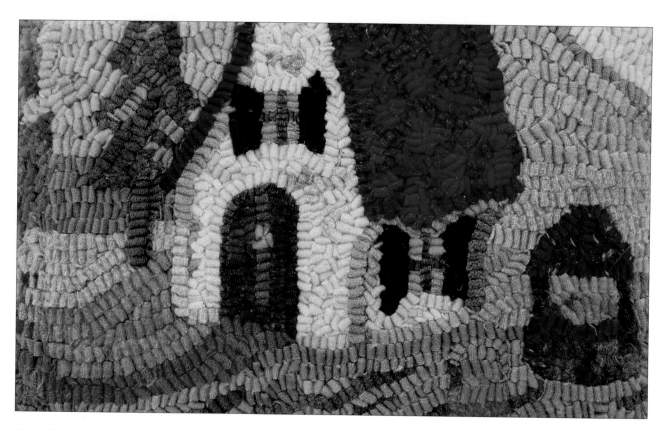

Kim Kaelin *thought* about rug hooking 18 years ago when her son was just a baby. "I made a mental note that I'd love to do that some day, if I ever had more time," she said. Years later, she moved to Minnesota, took a rug hooking class at a local quilt shop, and has been making rugs ever since.

Living by a lake in Minnesota where it's always snowy, sandy, or muddy, Kim decided to create a footstool to get her rug off a potentially dirty floor. She chose patterns from the *Hooking for Habitat* collection, designed by Terri Schaefer to benefit Habitat for Humanity. Together, the patterns represent the four seasons and incorporate features from her own home.

Cottage House (top), designed by Faith Williston, represents her house in the spring when the grass greens and the lake is free of ice. *Gingerbread House*, by Jennifer Roddewig, brings to mind the house decorated for the holidays. *Fish Shanty*, by Chris Savoy, reminds her of the ice fishing shacks on the frozen lake. *House Boat*, designed by Paulette Wentzlaff, represents the lazy summer days spent tubing and fishing. *Tree House*, designed by Melissa Elliott, showcases her backyard in autumn.

To unite the individual patterns, Kim pulled color from one element (the white aspen on one side) into another element (the ice shack on the adjoining side).

"Gifting the piece to my mother, who appreciates both its design and color, and the comfort it brings to her legs, is the icing on the cake."

KIM KAELIN
STILLWATER, MINNESOTA

For Kim—a mother, homemaker, and artist—rug hooking provides a bit of relaxation at the end of each day. She often designs her own patterns and finds dyeing wool to be one of her favorite steps in the rug hooking process. Her work, which often includes proddy, has won awards at the Minnesota State Fair. Kim sells her finished pieces at a Hudson, Wisconsin, art gallery and through her website, www.fancylegsfolkart.com.

In the Judges' Words

- *This stool makes me smile. The playful prodded fringe is a nice touch.*
- *Interesting idea and put together well.*
- *A charming piece.*

Hooking for Habitat Cube, 12" x 12" x 12", #6- to 8-cut hand-dyed wool on linen covering unfinished cube stool. Hooking for Habitat collection by Terri Schaefer with patterns designed by Melissa Elliott, Paulette Wentzlaff, Jennifer Roddewig, Faith Williston, and Chris Savoy; hooked by Kim Kaelin, Stillwater, Minnesota, 2009. PHOTO BY INSTUDIO

Jefferson Davis

Helen Lynch found herself in the right spot at the right time. "I drove a friend to Peg Hannum's rug hooking class," she said. "Rather than sitting idle for the whole time, I joined the class and began by hooking a pear chair seat. I was 'hooked.'"

Helen finished a number of smaller pieces in the following years, but *Jefferson Davis*, which measures over 8 1/2' wide, is only the second rug she's attempted. The pattern, designed by Pearl McGown, was inspired by an antique needlepoint rug at the Jefferson Davis museum in Montgomery, Alabama. Helen was drawn to the fine shading, the brilliant reds, and the challenge of hooking flowers.

Helen asked Nancy Blood to color plan the rug. The background wool is a spot dye, hooked in a meandering pattern to make the best use of its random coloring. The wool for the flowers and leaves was dyed in eight-value swatches.

For Helen, the most difficult part of the rug to execute—the flowers—was also her favorite. "I had never hooked flowers," she said. "Trying to replicate the roses was most challenging." At Peg Hannum's suggestion, she combined two eight-value swatches to shade the pedulas in the upper left and lower right corners, a combination that made those flowers her favorite elements of the rug.

Helen corded and whipped the edges in matching black yarn. The finished rug is displayed in her bedroom, "where my two greyhounds cannot 'pick' the roses."

In the Judges' Words

- *Beautiful roses.*
- *Exquisite color plan.*
- *Shading in the flowers is amazing.*

HELEN LYNCH
GLENMOORE, PENNSYLVANIA

Helen, a retired secondary math teacher, marks several firsts with Jefferson Davis: her first attempt at hooking flowers, her first experience with dyeing wool, and her first award for a hand-hooked rug. Helen is a member of Lancaster's Conestoga Chapter of the Pearl McGown Rugkrafters Guild.

Jefferson Davis, 46″ x 82″, #3-cut Dorr wool on linen.
Designed by Pearl McGown; hooked by Helen B. Lynch, Glenmoore,
Pennsylvania, 2010. PHOTO BY BILL BISHOP, IMPACT XPOSURES

Jungle Cat

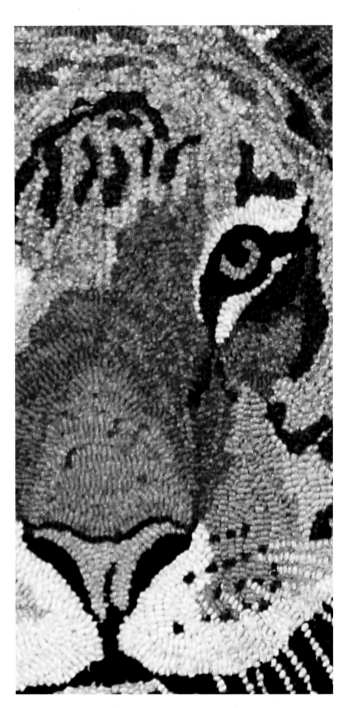

Cathy Sears had a bit of a rocky start with rug hooking. Her first project was an ambitious 33" by 37" mat that she color planned from bags and bags of recycled wool during an evening class. At the close of the eight-class session, she was only partway finished and completely overwhelmed. The unfinished mat ended up in her closet.

Six years later, Cathy decided to try again when a small rug hooking group started in her town. This time she started with smaller projects, working her way up to eventually finishing her first project. "I have been hooking ever since," she said.

Jungle Cat turned out to be another challenging rug for Cathy. She saw the pattern at a rug school on a silent auction table and knew she wanted to hook it because of the look in the tiger's eye.

Jon Ciemiewicz color planned the rug and dyed the wool for the project using regular, spot, and dip dyes. Cathy supplemented his choices with over-dyed hound's-tooth, herringbone, and plaids from her own stash.

Cathy began hooking *Jungle Cat*, but put the mat aside after she had finished about two thirds of the work to attend another workshop that included starting a new rug. "I had to really focus to start up on *Jungle Cat* again," she said. "And then I started to second-guess my wool choices. In the end I went with my instinct and just hooked it and gave myself a deadline to finish by."

In the Judges' Words

- *Well shaded, very lifelike.*
- *Pleasing directional hooking of face contour.*
- *The tiger looks like he could strike at any time.*

CATHY SEARS
ANTIGONISH, NOVA SCOTIA, CANADA

Cathy, a retired nurse, enjoys hooking a wide variety of patterns and experimenting with nontraditional materials like sari silk, yarn, and fleece. She has been hooking for six years and has completed eight smaller projects and six larger mats and wall hangings. She attends workshops and rug hooking schools and is a member of her local chapter of the Rug Hooking Guild of Nova Scotia. Cathy's inclusion in Celebration is her first rug hooking award.

Jungle Cat, 16" x 20", #5- and 6-cut wool on linen.
Designed by Jon Ciemiewicz; hooked by Cathy Sears, Antigonish, Nova Scotia, Canada, 2010. PHOTO BY CLAIRE MACLEAN

Large Frost Oriental

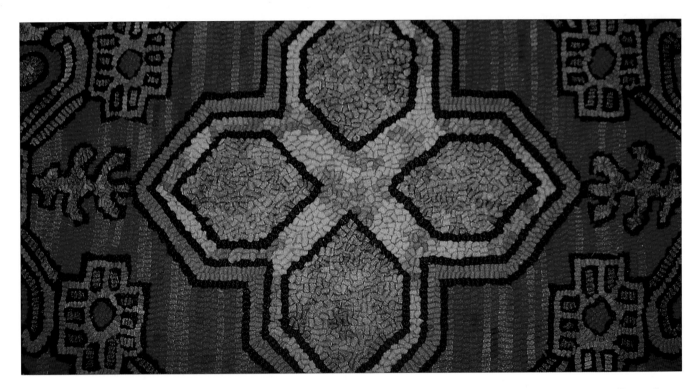

Nancy Parcels hooked this rug as a tribute to her mentor, Yvonne Miller. "She often said how *Large Frost Oriental* was her favorite Oriental design," Nancy said, "but she had never hooked it herself."

Nancy color planned her rug under the helpful watch of June Mikoryak, who chose the center field colors from Nancy's stash of dyed wool. June also taught Nancy a technique called annagodlyn, or meandering, to make the blue and tan wool in the center field appear to move and shimmer.

To get the colors she wanted, Nancy casserole dyed new and recycled wools. She used antique paisley for some of the details and also included a striped wool cut on the weft. To give her rug the look and feel of an antique Oriental carpet, she hooked in straight rows to mimic the back-and-forth motion of a weaver. In areas where straight line hooking

would have been difficult, she applied the annagodlyn technique.

During the two years that Nancy worked on this rug, she filled a notebook with color plans, formulas, and late night ideas. If you look closely at Nancy's rug, you might find the seven hidden messages she hooked into the rug. The pumpkin in the corner symbolizes that the rug was finished on Halloween, and she hooked the square around her middle initial in paisley in remembrance of Yvonne. Other secrets include her age, the date of completion in Roman numerals, three crosses hooked in paisley, a happy face, and a bar code.

In the Judges' Words

- *Interesting use of beading around the center motif.*
- *Colors and execution make for a lovely antique-looking rug.*
- *Looks like an expensive Oriental rug.*

NANCY Z. PARCELS
MECHANICSBURG, PENNSYLVANIA

Nancy pulled her first loop in 1999 and has hooked nearly 30 rugs and smaller mats to date. Currently she is fascinated by the prospect of hooking geometric and Oriental rugs. While she often hooks with #6 and #7 cuts, she has also been known to use other widths in her rugs. Nancy is a McGown certified teacher and belongs to a number of rug hooking organizations. This is her fourth rug to be featured in Celebration.

Large Frost Oriental, 37" x 72", #3-, 4-, and 5-cut wool and paisley on linen.
Designed by E. S. Frost; hooked by Nancy Z. Parcels, Mechanicsburg, Pennsylvania, 2010.

Mae Morris

Chizuko Hayami enjoys fine shading and was able to showcase her love of that technique in this classic pattern by William Morris, an English textile designer during the mid 1800s. She finds that many of Morris's rug, tapestry, and wallpaper designs translate beautifully into hooked rugs—and *Mae Morris* was no exception.

"I tried to express his world with minimum colors," she says. "Just blue, green, white, and a little bit of yellow."

Chizuko wanted her hooked rug to appear delicate and feathery, so she used #3-cut wool to take advantage of the fine-cut shading techniques. She dyed her own colors, choosing a dip dye for most of the shades. She created the yellow at the flowers' centers and the olive stems and borders with a casserole dye. The white in the rug is undyed Dorr Natural wool.

One lesson that Chizuko learned for future rugs is to cut her wool lengths for dyeing longer than she thinks necessary. "I measured and cut the wool four times the length then dip-dyed, but many times I didn't have enough length," she says. "Next time, longer lengths will make me hook easier and faster."

Chizuko doesn't enjoy sewing and often finds finishing her rugs a challenge. For *Mae Morris*, a bit of braiding tape and colored cord added a subtle flair and helped to conceal the backing at the folded edges. The finished rug hangs on the front wall at the entryway of her home.

In the Judges' Words

- *Beautifully hooked and nicely finished.*
- *Excellent shading and color choice.*
- *Pleasing color, beautiful shading.*

CHIZUKO HAYAMI
TOKYO, JAPAN

Chizuko Hayami lived in New York for five years and studied rug hooking and dyeing there with the late Dorothy Lotto. In the past 21 years, she has hooked more than 100 rugs. A McGown certified teacher, Chizuko is a member of the National Guild of Pearl K. McGown Rug Hookrafters and the Rug Hooking Guild of Nova Scotia. Her rugs were featured in Celebration XX and XVIII, and Mae Morris won People's Choice at the Northern McGown Teachers' Workshop exhibit.

Mae Morris, *33″ x 64^1/$_2$″, #3-cut Dorr wool on Scottish burlap.*
Designed by Jane McGown Flynn based on a William Morris design; hooked by Chizuko Hayami, Setagaya, Tokyo, Japan, 2010.

Mandarin Riches

Sometimes a pattern and a piece of wool just seem to be made for one another. That was the case when Pamela Schmelzle accepted an assignment to complete *Mandarin Riches* as a study in fret work for a teachers' class. Immediately, Pamela thought of a large piece of royal blue wool that Kay Hyde had given her more than a year earlier. "It was perfect for the background of the rug," she said.

To choose the colors for the flowers and the fret work, Pamela studied one of her mother's authentic Oriental carpets. She then jar dyed new white wool using Jewel Tones formulas by Carolyn Clemens.

After 40 years of rug hooking, Pamela knows that she doesn't enjoy hooking repetitive elements, so she was concerned about the border, one of four types of fret work common to Chinese Orientals. Her careful attention to detail was rewarded with sharp edges and straight lines.

Another difficult area for Pamela to hook was the background. About one third of the way through hooking the blue,

she noticed that the background was starting to ripple. "I was unknowingly hooking one row just slightly higher than the next," she said. Again, careful attention to each loop paid off with straight, even rows. "No matter how long you've hooked rugs, it's important to concentrate on your technique. You can prevent a lot of problems you might create for yourself."

Pamela's finished rug covers a portion of her bedroom floor and serves as a constant remembrance of her fellow rug hooker and friend, Kay Hyde.

In the Judges' Words

- *Beautifully shaded.*
- *The blue background makes the floral design pop.*

PAMELA SCHMELZLE
WAUTOMA, WISCONSIN

Working with wool is a tradition among the women in Pamela's family. Her grandmother dyed and braided wool to create floor rugs, and she learned to hook rugs from her mother. A retired nurse, Pamela is an accredited McGown instructor, a member of ATHA, and is active in her area guilds. She teaches from her home and at rug schools nationwide. Mandarin Riches is her first rug to be featured in Celebration.

Mandarin Riches, 26" x 42", #3-cut Dorr wool on linen. Designed by
Jane McGown Flynn; hooked by Pamela Moreman Schmelzle, Wautoma, Wisconsin, 2010. PHOTO BY GARY LABOUTON/LABOUTON PHOTOGRAPHY

Mountain Treeline

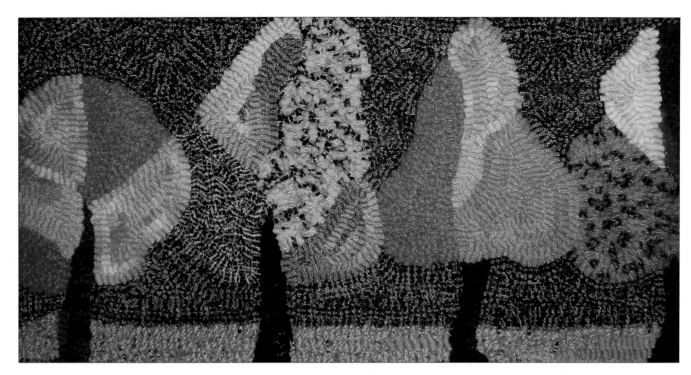

Susan Feller set her goals high with *Mountain Treeline*. While the outlined pattern may look simple, Susan's finished piece is anything but. "I wanted to achieve a change in planes," she said, "progressing from a detailed foreground to a deep field, then to distant hills with the skyline the farthest away."

Susan chose a pattern inspired by stained glass artist Anne-Renee Livingston, and drew her own inspiration from her favorite season, fall. She paired shades of dip-dyed red, yellow, orange, and green wool to duplicate the mix of leaf colors often seen on deciduous trees in the fall. She repeated the colors randomly in the foreground of the rug to suggest a carpet of colored leaves covering the earth.

To create the illusion of depth, Susan chose a dark, textured wool for the mountain behind the trees. A lighter colored wool makes the mountain at the upper left edge of the hooking recede into the distance.

Susan heightened the illusion of depth by dyeing a single piece of wool for the sky. She folded the wool then dip dyed it to achieve slight variations in the yellow color. "Even though I chose a very light value, I still felt hooking even in a #3 or #4 cut would distract from the other hooked, textured effects," she said. So instead of cutting the wool into strips, she cut the wool to fit the shape of the sky and hand stitched the fabric to the mountain line.

She stretched the finished piece around artist stretcher bars so it could hang on a wall without a wooden frame.

In the Judges' Words

- *Beautiful interpretation of a stylized design.*
- *Creatively finished.*
- *Bright colors are tastefully done.*

SUSAN FELLER
AUGUSTA, WEST VIRGINIA

Susan Feller learned knitting, crocheting, and hand sewing as a child from her mother and grandmother. Her love of rug hooking didn't develop until she was in her early 40s and had earned a degree in art and opened her own art gallery. Today, Susan runs Ruckman Mill Farm, exhibits her works both in the United States and abroad, teaches frequently, and writes about her artwork. Her rugs have appeared in Celebration X and XVI.

Mountain Treeline, 24" x 12", #6-cut hand-dyed wool and wool yarn on monk's cloth.
Designed by Anne-Renee Livingston, Ruckman Mill Farm; hooked by Susan L. Feller, Augusta, West Virginia, 2010.

November

An avid gardener, Lona Gabree learned to hook by working with Laurice Heath on her #6-cut primitive cat, but she soon realized that bringing forth finely shaded flowers and leaves would be her passion in rug hooking.

Lona chose *November* because the design reminded her of New England's pine trees and the crunch of crisp fall leaves underfoot, something she seldom experiences in her current home in Harahan, Louisiana. She started the rug at the 2008 Green Mountain Rug School under the guidance of Nancy Blood.

Nancy did both the color planning and the dyeing for Lona's rug, choosing 8-value swatches for #3-cut wool. They discussed an antique black background, but Nancy surprised Lona with peacock blue wool instead. "I was then out of my comfort zone," she said, "but realized after the first round of outlining my leaves just how gorgeous the blend of colors was. I learned to broaden my horizons."

Because Lona suffers from arthritis in her wrists, she used a haphazard pull of #3- and 4-cut strips to complete the background. She hired Rugs Finally Finished to whip and bind the edges in matching blue yarn and twill tape.

Lona's favorite part of the rug is the central motif because it includes "a leaf of every kind, all bouncing to life in the vibrant colors of a New England fall. I feel a deep sense of home each time I see *November*."

LONA GABREE
HARAHAN, LOUISIANA

Lona grew up on a New England farm but moved to Louisiana shortly after Hurricane Katrina so she and her husband could help with the efforts to rebuild the area. She enjoys a variety of fiber arts but focuses mainly on rug hooking and gardening now because of arthritis in her wrists. Lona has hooked 28 rugs and 2 wall hangings since learning the craft in 2003. November is her first rug to be featured in Celebration.

In the Judges' Words

- *Stunning colors and excellent placement.*
- *Background adds interest.*
- *The shading is lovely.*

November, 36" x 55", #3- and 4-cut wool on monk's cloth.
Designed by Pearl McGown; hooked by Lona Gabree, Harahan, Louisiana, 2010. PHOTO BY LOUIS, NEW ORLEANS, LA

Osiris

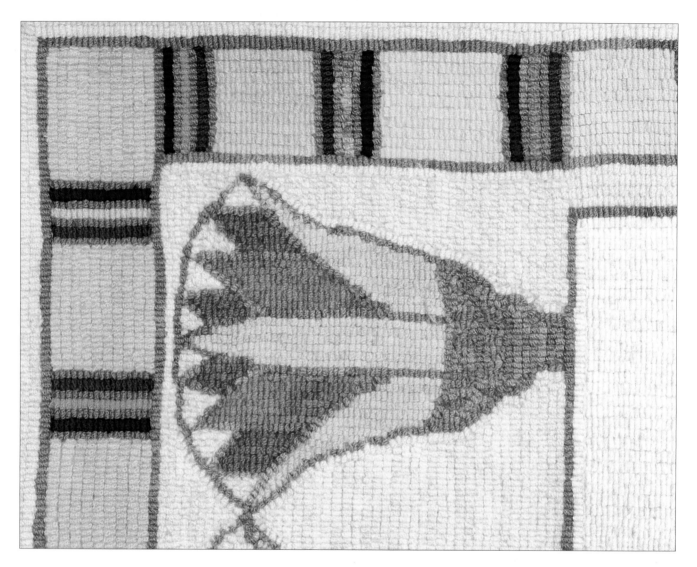

Corinne Bridge has always been interested in ancient crafts. When she saw this Egyptian-inspired design in the House of Price catalog, she knew it would be the ideal pattern for her next rug hooking project.

Corinne purchased the pattern then let it sit while she attended several rug hooking workshops and camps. "I had in mind what colors I liked and started collecting them during my trips," she said.

Corinne purchased the dark blue color around the baby vultures and paired it with a deep blue-turquoise and a lighter turquoise spot dye for the wings. The lotus colors were swatches in various shades of a pink carnelian. She chose two versions of sand for the light backgrounds and hooked the orbs with graduated gold. To give the rug the look and feel of

ancient Egyptian artwork, Corinne outlined each element in the center field in gold.

The rug's finishing touches presented the most problems for Corinne. She bought the bright-colored wools from Anne Eastwood but ran out. "I had to dye and redye several times to get the proper match," she said. Corinne also had trouble finding a suitable spot for the date and her initials. "There seemed to be no appropriate location, so I added the cartouches," she said. "I could have used Roman numerals, XXM, but that would not have been Egyptian!"

Corinne finished the rug with a technique she developed. She folded over the linen, notched the corners, and prepared a long strip of 2½-inch wool to cover the fold.

CORINNE BRIDGE
LARGO, FLORIDA

Corinne started hooking rugs in 1954 when she attended an adult education class taught by Estelle Rathbun. In 2000, she was able to turn her on-again, off-again rug hooking habit into a full-time vocation. Corinne prefers to hook in #3 and #4 cuts and enjoys using a stained glass technique she learned from Ingrid Heironimus. She is a member of ATHA and has won numerous ribbons at local and state fairs. Osiris is her first Celebration rug.

Osiris, 20" x 44", #3- and 4-cut wool on linen. Designed by House of Price; hooked by Corinne M. Bridge, Largo, Florida, 2010. PHOTO BY JERRY LUCAS

Persian Miniature

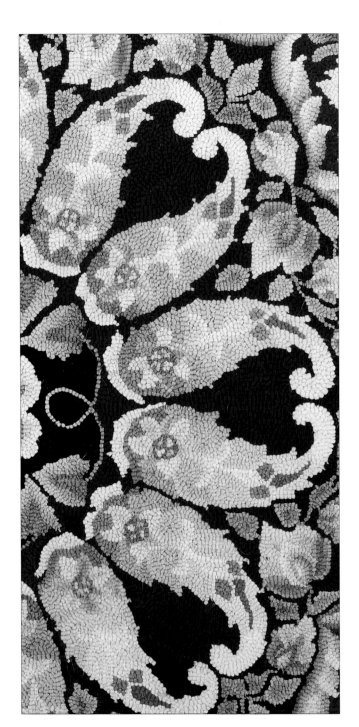

Mystical forces may have been behind Cheryl Meese's decision to hook *Persian Miniature*. "I frequently look through a fairly tall pile of past issues [of *Rug Hooking* magazine and *News & Views*] for help, ideas, and inspiration so they should have been well shuffled," she said. "But for some reason the January 1992 issue featuring Carol Kassera's *Persian Miniature* was always on the top of the pile."

Cheryl took the magazine's prominent and perpetual placement as a sign and asked Carol to color plan the rug for her. Carol used dip, casserole, gradation, and spot dyes to create a vibrant color palette that Cheryl found inspiring.

Cheryl's favorite part of the rug is the floral area of the medallion, between the central paisleys and the ivory background. "I loved doing all the different flowers and the leaves," she said. "Each was complicated but small enough to be a good—but not overwhelming—challenge."

Given the size of the rug—nearly four feet by five feet—simply completing the rug became Cheryl's biggest challenge. She started *Persian Miniature* in October 2001, hooked on and off over the next eight years, then realized that she'd need a plan if she hoped to finish it in the same decade. "I divided the uncompleted parts into the number of months I had left," she said. "Each small area was manageable and less overwhelming."

Since completing the rug, Cheryl reports that the January 1992 issue of RHM has mysteriously disappeared into the depths of her back issues stack.

In the Judges' Words

- *Well balanced color in this rug.*
- *Excellent technique.*
- *Lovely colors.*

CHERYL MEESE
DULUTH, MINNESOTA

Cheryl is a stockbroker and certified financial planner who has been hooking rugs for almost 30 years. She has completed 14 rugs, some rather large, as well as pillows and ornaments. She prefers fine shading and gravitates toward Oriental patterns. However she recently tried her hand at a portrait of her two dogs and a pictorial. Persian Miniature is her second rug to be featured in Celebration. Her Queen Mary rug appeared in Celebration XIV.

Persian Miniature, 50″ x 60″, #3- and 4-cut hand-dyed wool on monk's cloth.
Designed by Pearl McGown; hooked by Cheryl Meese, Duluth, Minnesota, 2010. PHOTO BY FIFIELD PORTRAIT DESIGNS

Saraphina

Jill Walker is not one to back away from a challenge. When she decided to hook *Saraphina*, she started with the most difficult area of the rug—the mermaid's face. "Getting the shading right on the planes of her face was the most challenging part of this rug," Jill said. "I met the challenge by hooking it over, and over, and over. . ."

Jill started *Saraphina* in a mini-class taught by Pris Buttler. She was captivated by the subject matter and the colors that Pris had used in her fun and unique version of the rug. To color plan the rug, Jill borrowed heavily from Pris' finished piece and incorporated some wool she had in her stash to round out the design. She dyed swatches for the mermaid's skin and the water bubbles, and used spot dyes in the background and border.

Jill used mostly new wool with a few over-dyed, found pieces of wool. Being a needle worker as well as a rug hooker, Jill couldn't resist working some Kreinik filament into the mermaid's hair, scales, and bubbles to create a subtle glimmer.

Her favorite part of the rug is the mermaid's hair. "I enjoyed getting the color mix just right and making it look tangled and floating, but not too wild and messy," she said. "It was difficult to get the right balance."

In the end, Jill was thrilled with her finished piece. "I learned it's worth taking the time to do it right," she said, "even if that means ripping sections out and putting it away for a few months."

In the Judges' Words

- *A charming hooked piece.*
- *Good hooking technique and nicely finished.*
- *Very nice facial shading and expression.*

JILL WALKER
WEST SACRAMENTO, CALIFORNIA

Jill, a graphic designer by trade, believes it "took a village to make me the rug hooker I am today." She studied with a number of teachers, attended classes at the Cambria Pines Rug Camp, and has easy access to wool from some of the best dyers in the rug hooking community. She is a member of the Camellia City Rug Hooking Guild and has won a number of ribbons at the California State Fair.

Saraphina, 19″ x 27″, #4-, 5-, and 6-cut wool on monk's cloth.
Designed by Pris Buttler; hooked by Jill Walker, West Sacramento, California, 2009.

Shah Abbas

Susan Grant struck a deal with her sister, Shirley Davies: "I'll make you a rug if you make me a quilt." Her sister agreed, and Susan chose *Shah Abbas* to match the décor of the renovated general store where her sister lives.

To color plan the rug, Susan first chose colors for the three medallions in the center field. Using dye formulas by Barbie Baker-Dykens, she spot and dip dyed her sister's favorite colors then dyed transitional swatches for the shaded elements within the medallions and the border. The tan background uses spot dyes, dip dyes, and abrashed wool.

Susan was surprised to find that the thin blue borders around the medallions and at the inside corners were the most difficult areas of the rug to hook. "Believe it or not, making them match each other was hard," she said.

The peacock blue flowers in the medallions were Susan's favorite part of the rug. She alternated the shading of the

repeating motifs, which lent a fun, unexpected touch—and a surprise—to those who look closely at the finished piece.

Susan whipped the edges of the rug with wool yarn and finished the rug with binding tape. The 6½-foot-wide rug now covers part of the main floor of her sister's house.

The quilt that Susan received in trade is done in shades of purple, rose, and a light but vibrant green. "She was much faster than I was and had the quilt ready long before I had finished the rug for her," Susan said.

SUSAN GRANT
GEORGETOWN, ONTARIO, CANADA

Inspired by a fellow high school teacher, Susan decided to try her hand at rug hooking when she retired from teaching high school in 2004. Over the past seven years, Susan has hooked pillows, a Christmas stocking, wall hangings, and rugs, finding that her pieces grow bigger as she gains more experience. She is a member of the Georgetown Rug and the Ontario Hooking craft guilds. Her inclusion in Celebration XXI *is her first rug hooking award.*

In the Judges' Words

- *Lovely abrash center background.*
- *Well executed with good color movement and background.*
- *Very nicely executed rug.*

Shah Abbas, 40" x 78", #3-, 4-, and 5-cut hand-dyed wool on rug warp.
Designed by Jane McGown Flynn; hooked by Susan Grant, Georgetown, Ontario, Canada, 2010. PHOTO BY KRISTEN HARRISON

Sleuthing

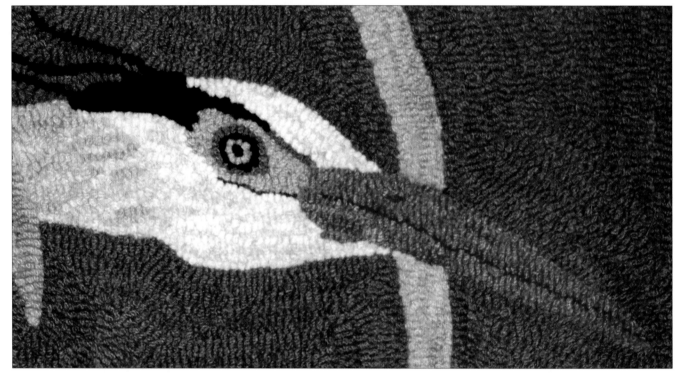

G illian Tomkins was drawn to this pattern of a great blue heron because of its photographic-like qualities. "I wanted to hook the bird as realistically as possible," she said.

In order to accomplish her goal, Gillian used a number of reference photos showing various poses and angles of the great blue heron in its natural habitat. "Working on this rug really showed me the importance of using as many visuals as possible when hooking realistic figures."

Gillian's teacher, Katie Puckett, color planned the rug and presented Gillian with a bundle of spot, dip, and over-dyed plaid and plain wool. Swatches were used for the shaded areas of the bird and the vegetation.

The most difficult parts of the rug to hook were the wing feathers. "I must have hooked and re-hooked at least three times," she said. Gillian's visual references came in very handy during this stage, as did the pointers on adding detail that were offered by her teacher.

Gillian's favorite aspect is the way the colors transition between the head and the neck, and the eye. "I love the way the eye is looking at you . . . watching you as if you are disturbing it while it is feeding," she said.

Gillian finished the rug with cording, a whipped edge, and binding tape. The completed rug holds a place of honor in her studio, where Gillian can work under the heron's watchful eye.

In the Judges' Words

- *Simple background really makes the bird the focus of the rug.*
- *Well shaded.*
- *The blue background is a nice choice to highlight the crane and leaves.*

GILLIAN TOMKINS
PONTE VEDRA BEACH, FLORIDA

Gillian Tomkins limits her involvement in fiber arts to just one—rug hooking—in an attempt to control the amount of worms and snippets in her home. She started hooking rugs in 2007 after attending a rug camp at the local bead store where Beverly Conway was teaching. Gillian has attended the Off the Ocean Rug Hooking Conference in Jacksonville, Florida, for the past four years. Sleuthing is her second rug to be featured in Celebration.

Sleuthing, 35³/₄″ x 20¹/₂″, #3-cut wool on monk's cloth.
Designed by Beverly Conway; hooked by Gillian Tomkins, Ponte Vedra Beach, Florida, 2009. PHOTO BY RAYMOND TOMKINS

Square Harmony

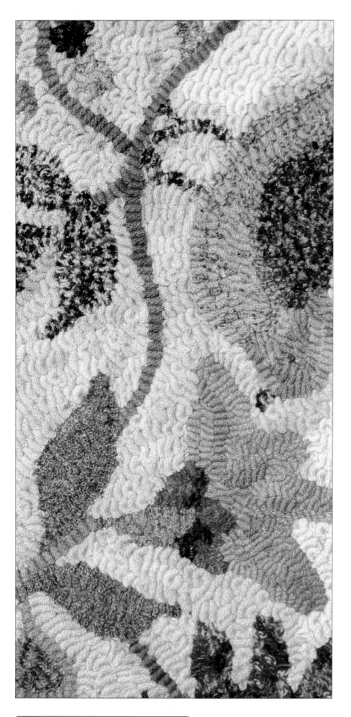

Nancy fell in love with this rug when she saw that her friend Nancy Butts Thompson had hooked it first. "My friend hooked her rug in pastels and bright colors," a color scheme that didn't appeal to Nancy. "But this rug talked to me," she said.

Jeanne Benjamin color planned the rug, using the subtler and more antique-like colors that Nancy adores. She chose a cream background to make the colors of the flowers, the birds, and the squares stand out. Jeanne also dyed the wool for the rug. She used spot dyes, a casserole dye, and some dip dyes over new and recycled wool to create the variety of colors Nancy needed for all the different elements.

The most challenging part of completing this rug was dealing with the color plan that Jeanne delivered. "I have never had a color plan as detailed as this rug was," Nancy said. "It was just overwhelming." Nancy worked steadily on one small area of the rug at a time, and with great encouragement from Jeanne and her fellow rug hookers at Caraway Camp, she successfully completed the rug.

Nancy whipped the edges of the finished rug with yarn that Sheri Bennett dyed to match the background. She used a piece of background wool in place of the tape on the back of the rug.

Nancy placed the completed rug in her master bath. "It's in an area where water is not a problem, and it's the first thing you see as you enter the bathroom," she said.

In the Judges' Words

- *Colors relate well to one another.*
- *Lively color combinations.*
- *Very nice use of textures.*

NANCY DIEGEL
OOLTEWAH, TENNESSEE

Nancy Diegel credits her interest in rug hooking to one woman: Ramona Maddox. "I met Ramona in the early 1970s," Nancy said. "She made such an impression while she was hooking The Lord's Supper *that I knew I eventually wanted to learn this art." Nancy has been hooking since 2003 and has completed 30 pieces of artwork. She exhibits her work regionally.* Square Harmony *is her first rug to be included in Celebration.*

Square Harmony, 52″ x 33³/4″, #6-cut wool on linen.
Designed by Monika Jones; hooked by Nancy Diegel, Ooltewah, Tennessee, 2009. <small>PHOTO BY LANGSTON PHOTOGRAPHY</small>

Sultan

In the 17 years she's been rug hooking, Susan Minorini has yet to hook a rug she likes more than *Sultan*. "I love Orientals, especially Persian Orientals," Susan said. "With *Sultan*, I love the design of the flowers and the border. It's not a cluttered design."

And to top it all off, Susan says it wasn't a challenge to hook, either. "The design was copied 'straight on the grain,' so I didn't have to adjust the lines," she said. Because she liked the colors so much, she didn't even make any adjustments to the color plan.

Susan chose the color combination for *Sultan* at an exhibit where she watched John Ewbank hook one of his own designs in blue, red, and gold on a dark background. As she talked with John, he mentioned that Nancy Blood had helped him to color plan his rug. After writing a letter to Nancy, Susan had the for-

mulas in hand to dye her own wool in those same colors.

To give the rug a dark, rich look, Susan opted to spot dye the colors instead of using the swatches she had seen John working with. She over dyed new, colored wool to enhance the effect. "Dyeing over white or natural wool would have made for brighter colors," she said. She hooked the background in straight rows to mimic a woven Oriental rug.

Susan whipped the edges of her rug, and the finished piece now hangs on the wall of her living room.

In the Judges' Words

- *Colors make a nice graphic statement.*
- *Excellent technique.*
- *Colors are striking and well balanced.*

SUSAN MINORINI
LAKE BLUFF, ILLINOIS

Susan, a retired teacher, took her first lessons in rug hooking from Albert Swift in 1994. She is comfortable hooking in all widths but prefers to work with #3, #4, and #5 cuts. Susan is a McGown certified teacher, chairman of activities and members at large of the National Guild of Pearl K. McGown Hookrafters, and Assistant Director of the McGown Teachers' Workshop Northern Division. Sultan's inclusion in Celebration XXI is her first rug hooking award.

Sultan, 37" x 54", #3- and 4-cut wool on rug warp.
Designed by Selma Dhanji; hooked by Susan Minorini, Lake Bluff, Illinois, 2009. PHOTO BY KATHY WEINSTEIN PHOTOGRAPHY

SHOWCASE OF

Adaptation Designs

ADAPTATION

A rug hooked as a copy or interpretation of a piece of work originally found in another medium. A re-creation of another's painting, photograph, postcard, or art.

A Sunday Afternoon on the Island of La Grande Jatte

Karen Whidden has always been captivated by impressionist paintings and how the artists manage to capture an interpretation of the visible world rather than an exact duplicate. Her goal in hooking Georges-Pierre Seurat's *A Sunday Afternoon on the Island of La Grande Jatte* was to see how well wool could mimic the artist's depiction of a silent and graceful moment in time.

Karen used only Dorr Natural 100% wool—no plaids, striped, textured, or recycled wools. She then dyed all the wool using straight, spot, and over dyeing techniques. "I found so many different color variations [in my research], so I decided to use colors that I felt best captured the sentiment of the original painting."

For Karen, the most challenging part of designing this rug was incorporating the more than 50 people, animals, and objects from the original painting. Sometimes she needed to hook a full figure; other times a few loops of color in the right place did the job perfectly.

One of those spots where minimal loops made a maximum impact is along the left edge of the rug. There, just above the reclining man's leg, is a miniscule ladybug. A collector of ladybug artifacts, Karen tries to include a tiny version of her favorite insect in all her rug designs.

After just over a month of planning and hooking, Karen finished the rug. She hooked a mottled blue, thin border and finished the edges with dark blue binding tape. "The color and width seemed to frame the rug without creating any distraction."

In the Judges' Words

- *People are hard to hook; she did it with ease over and over again.*
- *Reflects a good rendition of the original.*
- *Pleasant color balance.*

KAREN WHIDDEN
SOUTHERN PINES, NORTH CAROLINA

Karen became fascinated with traditional rug hooking when she and her husband retired to the warmer regions of North Carolina. Now she does most of her rug hooking in the evening while she and her husband watch television. Karen is a member of the McGown guild, ATHA, and the Sandhills Rug Artists. She has hooked more than 100 pieces, and exhibits and sells her work locally at Artist Alley. Sunday Afternoon is her fourth rug to appear in Celebration.

A Sunday Afternoon on the Island of La Grande Jatte, 36" x 26", #3-, 4-, and 5-cut wool on rug warp. *Adapted from a painting by Seurat (A Sunday Afternoon on the Island of La Grande Jatte) and hooked by Karen Whidden, Southern Pines, North Carolina, 2009.* PHOTO BY JOHN WHIDDEN

Bighorns

Roland Nunn chose this landscape scene because he likes the challenge of hooking animals in their natural setting. Bighorn sheep, like these two males, are found in the Rocky Mountain regions from Canada to northern Mexico and are often portrayed as symbols of strength and wilderness.

When working a landscape design—with or without animals—Roland points to swatches as the most important part of his rug hooking process. In *Bighorns*, Roland used 24 different swatches. "The use of a parent (base) swatch plus its transitional companions allows subtle variations in color with smooth transitions."

Roland's reference material for his hooked piece showed a clear blue sky. To add color and interest to the finished piece, he modified the scene to show a thunderstorm approaching from the left. That slight alteration changed the mood of his work from a simple, majestic portrait to one of elegance mixed with a sense of urgency.

Roland created the colors for the storm clouds by paintbrush dyeing a piece of wool. To enhance the variation among the colors, Roland reverse-hooked portions of the clouds.

Roland used swatches to shade the two bighorn sheep. In the wild, the colors of their hides are very close to those of the landscape, but Roland didn't want them to disappear into the background of the rug. Their bold stance and the shadows underneath their bodies assure that the sheep are the focus of the piece.

"Each time I hook a new landscape, the experience gained helps make the next one easier," he said.

In the Judges' Words

- *Animals are well done.*
- *Contrast of values in the shadows adds so much to overall composition.*
- *Excellent detail.*

ROLAND NUNN
ORINDA, CALIFORNIA

When Roland turned 60, he decided he needed a "sit-down hobby." His mother had hooked rugs in the 1950s, so he turned to rug hooking as a possible pastime, and it stuck. In the past 20 years, Roland has hooked 56 rugs in all styles from landscapes to geometrics. His rugs have been featured in Celebration *six times—from honorable mention to the front cover—and have won a number of awards, including four best of shows.*

Bighorns, 24″ x 32″, #3-cut wool on monk's cloth. Adapted from a photo and hooked by Roland Nunn, Orinda, California, 2010.

Love on the Meadow

Beth Ann Gibbs keeps saying the next rug she hooks will be a dark primitive, and she's still saying it. Her latest rug, *Love on the Meadow*, certainly does not qualify as dark or primitive.

Beth Ann adapted one of her daughter's engagement pictures to create a wedding rug for Julie Anne and her fiancé, Andrew. She was captivated by the pose and the expression of the figures, and by their surroundings. Beth Ann used the photograph to color plan the rug and asked her teacher, Eric Sandberg, to tweak some of the individual colors and choose shades for the faces.

Once the color planning was done, Beth Ann spent several days dyeing the wool. She used three different casserole dyes to create the mottled variations of blue for the sky. The greens for the trees were made with casserole dyes, spot dyes, and dip dyes. Twelve different values of flesh tones dyed in different casseroles make up the colors of the faces.

Beth Ann also tried—and found success—with a new rug hooking technique. She used three strips of #3-cut wool in different colors, pulling all three through the same hole in the backing to give the foreground a blended effect.

Diagnosed with stage 4 cancer in 2003 and now in remission, Beth Ann noted how special this rug is. "When I realized my dream of seeing my daughter married would come true, my gift to her became that much more special. This rug is full of love, life, thanksgiving, and joy unmeasurable."

In the Judges' Words

- *Faces express emotion nicely.*
- *Excellent use of values and contrast to show depth.*
- *Clothing is so lifelike.*

BETH ANN GIBBS
KENNESAW, GEORGIA

Beth Ann's sister, Sandy, introduced her to rug hooking when Beth Ann was struggling with cancer. "The day she provided me with hook, frame, cutter, and wool was a lifesaver," she said. Beth Ann has hooked everything from mug rugs to a purse to more than 20 rugs in the past 8 years, and one of her first rugs won best of show at the Georgia State Fair. Love on the Meadow is her first rug to be featured in Celebration.

Love on the Meadow, 28" x 19", #3- to 6-cut wool on rug warp.
Adapted from a photo by Mark Elkins and hooked by Beth Ann Gibbs, Kennesaw, Georgia, 2010.

Mama Longhorn

Victoria Hart Ingalls' rug hooking teacher, Margaret Hunt Masters, once told Victoria never to hook from a photograph. She didn't understand why until she decided to use a small portion of a larger photograph to create Mama Longhorn.

"The whole piece was a challenge from the minute I started the sketch," she said. "It must be because one sees so many value changes in a photograph that have to be simplified when 'painting' with wool."

Victoria dyed the greens for the background in one pot, stirring as little as possible to achieve the mottled look she was after. For the cow and calf, she used several swatches dyed by Jane Olson.

While the realistic shading of the animals' hides was a challenge to duplicate, Victoria found the background to be the most difficult part of the rug to hook. "I didn't want to copy the photograph, which included trees, blue sky, and other cattle," she said. "I just wanted soft greens that would enhance the figures. I worked loop by loop, placing lights and darks carefully to soften some areas and bring others forward."

Victoria's husband framed the finished piece, stretching the hooking over a piece of padded foam core, then gluing the edges of the monk's cloth to the back. She chose the wide frame to complement the rich colors of the mother and her calf. "This portrait was my greatest artistic accomplishment in any medium," Victoria said. It commandeers a special place on her bedroom wall with all her other treasures.

In the Judges' Words

- *The animals are wonderful.*
- *Superb colors and excellent understanding of shading.*
- *What a sweet rug.*

VICTORIA HART INGALLS
INDEPENDENCE, MISSOURI

Rug hooking is a generational hobby for Victoria. She, her mother, and her grandmother all spent nearly a decade learning the art of rug hooking from Margaret Hunt Masters. Victoria herself has been hooking for 35 years and has hooked so many pieces that she's lost count. She enjoys working in #3- to 6-cut strips, but is most comfortable with fine shading and portraits. Mama Longhorn is her third rug to be accepted into Celebration.

Mama Longhorn, 11¹/₄" square, #3-cut wool on monk's cloth. Adapted from a photograph by Harland J. Schuster and hooked by Victoria Hart Ingalls, Independence, Missouri, 2010.
PHOTO BY E. TODD HOTTMAN

Something Old Something New

When Deborah Walsh met her stepmom and sister for their annual weekend hook-in, their challenge to her was to design a still life rug hooking. She immediately thought of an advertisement for an art show for her former boss, David Barba. "His watercolor *Something Old, Something New* was on the postcard and I fell in love with it," she said. "I thought the still life pattern of that piece would be a fun challenge."

After receiving permission from the artist, Deborah transferred the design to linen and ordered wool. Norma Batastini dyed some of the blue wool used in the bottles and the background wool; Michele Micarelli dyed the brightly colored wool for the flowers.

Deborah found the flowers to be the most challenging part of hooking this rug. To make her work a little easier and the hooking pattern a little cleaner, she simplified the number of flowers and greenery when she transferred the pattern to linen. Even with that modification, Deborah admits that she ended up rehooking some of the flowers several times until she got the shading and color play she wanted.

Deborah is pleased with the way all the pieces of this rug came together, and she especially likes the look of the bottles in the finished piece. Hooking the stems as they would be affected by the water and the glass was a challenge, as was making sure the glass itself looked realistic. "It is very rewarding to hook a rug based on a piece of art that you love," she said.

In the Judges' Words

- *Beautiful bright colors and well balanced.*
- *Good color movement and representation of glass.*
- *Superior finishing.*

DEBORAH WALSH
CRANFORD, NEW JERSEY

Deborah, a mom of three and a part-time behavioral therapist for autistic children, started rug hooking in 2000. Since then she has hooked 40 rugs and attended numerous workshops and classes. She finds herself gravitating toward hooking flowers and primitive pieces in #8-cut wool. Like the title of her piece, her entry in Celebration incorporates something old (her love of flowers) but uses something new (smaller strips). This is her first rug hooking award.

Something Old Something New, 36″ x 30″, #4- and 6-cut wool on linen.
Adapted from a painting by David Barba and hooked by Deborah Walsh, Cranford, New Jersey, 2010. PHOTO BY BILL BISHOP, IMPACT XPOSURES

To See the World in a Grain of Sand

Suzanne Gunn finds her three-year-old grandson to be a very pensive little boy. When she saw a photo of him playing on the gray sand beaches of New Zealand, she was compelled to capture not only the physical moment in time, but also Angus' emotions and thoughts as he gazed at the sand.

The most challenging part of creating this rug was not hooking the figure of her grandson but dyeing the wool for the gray sand. Her first attempt was too mottled, so she dyed the wool a second time for a more subtle effect. Suzanne achieved the gray she wanted, but unfortunately didn't dye enough wool. "It was harder than I thought to get the same gray," she says. "I am bad for not measuring, and I like to dye by eye, which can get you into trouble!"

Suzanne chose a thin metal frame to complement the hooked piece. The finished rug hangs in her husband's office and waiting rooms with several of her other rugs.

Almost all of the 63 rugs Suzanne has created over the past 16 years are portraits, which at one point led her to feel stagnant about her art. Her response was to try three underwater-themed rugs in mixed medium. "It was exciting and liberating to do something so completely different, but I missed my portraits. I plan to do more mixed medium, but the human figure is still it for me. What I learned from *To See the World in a Grain of Sand* is that I will always want to do figures."

In the Judges' Words

- *Beautifully captures a child's wonder.*
- *Little boy is exquisite.*
- *Excellent color balance.*

SUZANNE GUNN
CENTREVILLE, NOVA SCOTIA, CANADA

Suzanne taught herself to hook and for years used only commercial patterns. In 2004, she designed her first rug and found that hooking her own designs met all her artistic needs and more. Suzanne also created stained glass, watercolors, and oils, noting that painting has helped her to achieve the look she wants in her hooked rugs. Suzanne is a member of ATHA and the Square Zebras. Her rugs have been featured in Celebration four times.

To See the World in a Grain of Sand, 37" x 25", #3- and 4-cut new Dorr and Leicester wool on linen.
Adapted from a family photograph and hooked by Suzanne Gunn, Centreville, Nova Scotia, Canada, 2010.

Van Gogh's Twelve Sunflowers

When Sally sat down to design this adaptation of Vincent Van Gogh's painting *Still Life: Vase with Twelve Sunflowers*, her goal was to create a simple and straightforward replica. She drew the pattern, included a copy of the picture that was her inspiration, and sent everything to Cindi Gay for color planning.

"I could hardly wait to see all those beautiful oranges, yellows, rusts, and purples," she said. "This was to be my tribute to my favorite artist. A rug as nearly like the painting as I could make it."

As she worked, Sally found that hooking the sunflowers wasn't as simple or as straightforward as she'd imagined. Figuring out which petals belonged to which sunflower was a challenge. "After completing one and going to the next I would discover one or more petals attached to the wrong flower center, resulting in some serious reverse hooking."

Her favorite part of the rug is a flower lost in a tangle of orange petals near the bottom of the arrangement. After trying multiple times to hook that area without success, Sally picked up a magnifying glass to find that what she thought was a seed pod was actually another flower.

Sally was unable to match Van Gogh's painting stroke by stroke in the background, but found that her dream of a tribute to her favorite artist didn't suffer. "When doing an adaptation, one should never strive for a perfect match with the model," she said. "Instead of being a chore, hooking the background turned out to be an enjoyable part of the project."

SALLY KERR
KNOXVILLE, TENNESSEE

Sally started to hook rugs during a visit to Italy. Upon her return to the States, she learned shading, theory, and a list of dos and don'ts with Genevieve Patterson. Over the past 12 years, Sally has hooked numerous pillow tops, a handful of rugs, and a footstool cover. She finds hooking primitives to be relaxing, and she enjoys the challenge of using specially dyed wool in smaller strips. This rug is her first to be featured in Celebration.

Van Gogh's Twelve Sunflowers, 24¹/₂″ x 30″, #3- to 7-cut wool on linen.
Adapted from a painting by Van Gogh and hooked by Sally Kerr, Knoxville, Tennessee, 2009. PHOTO BY KEVAN KERR

ADAPTATION DESIGNS

Veterans Day

Donna Hrkman never planned to enjoy rug hooking. "My friend Alice Strebel of Kindred Spirits nagged me into trying it," she said. "I wasn't really interested in trying something new, but I finally gave in. I hooked a small primitive mat that I drew up myself and, of course, fell in love with hooking."

Her love of rug hooking led Donna to enter the 2010 Sauder Village Theme Challenge: Happy Holidays. Assuming many entrants would choose to portray scenes from the more widely celebrated holidays, like Christmas, Donna thought she would use a different holiday. "I opted for Veterans Day," she said. "I Googled images of soldiers, and this image of Joseph Ambrose holding a folded American flag while dressed in his old WWI uniform spoke to me."

Donna hooked the gentleman's face without any problem, working quickly to capture the mixture of pride, sadness, and regret that was revealed in the photograph. To accurately portray the shading and the colors in the uniform took more time. The background, which she changed several times until it no longer resembled the original photograph, took the most time.

Donna is especially proud of how the flag appears in the finished piece. "I wanted it to look three dimensional," she said. "It is the flag from his son's coffin; he was killed in the Korean War.

"For me, every new rug is a challenge," Donna said. "I always hook from the heart, and I want that to show in every rug I make."

In the Judges' Words

- *Face expresses great emotion.*
- *Directional hooking adds so much depth.*
- *Makes you think.*

DONNA HRKMAN
DAYTON, OHIO

In her nine years of rug hooking, Donna, a professional rug hooker and certified stencil artist, has switched from wide-cut primitive designs to smaller cuts like the #3s, 4s, and 5s used to create this portrait of a WWI soldier. Veterans Day won the people's choice ribbon in the theme challenge at Sauder Village in 2010, and three of Donna's other rugs have been featured in Celebration. She frequently writes for RHM.

Veterans Day, 29″ x 35″, #2- to 6-cut wool on linen.
Adapted from a photograph of Joseph Ambrose and hooked by Donna Hrkman, Dayton, Ohio, 2010.

Waging Peace, Fighting Disease, Building Hope

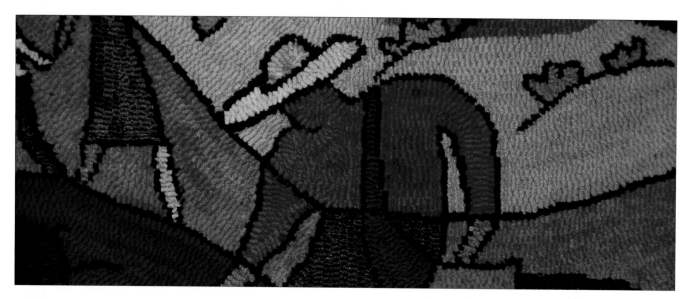

Susan Naples' rug, *Waging Peace, Fighting Disease, Building Hope*, fuses two of her passions: philanthropy and rug hooking.

Susan started with the artwork of Nip Rogers. His vibrant depiction of a Third World scene caught her eye when it was used on the cover of the 2007–2008 Annual Report of The Carter Center, a philanthropic organization based in Atlanta, Georgia, that promotes peace and healthy living conditions all over the world.

She chose rich colors from her large inventory of wool, supplementing them with additional purchases from Jane Olson and Diane Stoffel. She outlined each element as the artist had done in his original, then used directional hooking and echoing lines to further separate the elements. The shading is not subtle, but done in bold strokes to mimic the original artwork. "My work is usually quite detailed, hooked with #3, 4, and 5 cuts," she said. "This piece is a little more primitive than I usually hook."

Susan found it challenging to translate the painting to fiber while retaining the intensity of the emotion in the original piece of art. One of the most difficult areas to hook was where several loops portrayed the movement of water being poured into a jug.

"Creating the rug brought me so much joy that I didn't want its ability to inspire to stop there," she said. She donated the rug to be auctioned off by The Carter Center, raising $4,500 to help fund their fight to eliminate the parasitic Guinea worm and the diseases and conflicts that result from its infestations.

In the Judges' Words

- Bright colors, well placed.
- Effective attention to detail.
- All motifs very crisp.

SUSAN NAPLES
SANTA ANA, CALIFORNIA

Susan learned to hook from her aunt, Jan Leavitt, who had been hooking rugs for 50 years. When Susan discovered a vast array of hand-hooked rugs in her aunt's home, she "was enthralled, as was my aunt that I was interested, since she had raised four boys," Susan said. Over the past 17 years, she has hooked 30 rugs. Susan is a member of ATHA. This is her third rug to be featured in Celebration.

Waging Peace, Fighting Disease, Building Hope, 24" x 32", #3-cut wool on rug warp. *Adapted from Nip Rogers' cover art for the 2007–2008 Carter Center Annual Report and hooked by Susan Naples, Santa Ana, California, 2009.* PHOTO BY MARY WORTMAN

SHOWCASE OF

Honorable Mention

*Heat Wave, 32" x 56", #4-cut wool on linen. Designed by Frasier;
hooked by Erika A. DeCree, Quantico, Virginia, 2009.* PHOTO BY ANNETTE BAUDELOQUE

Dear Celebration Reader:

Which rugs are your favorites?

The judges have chosen the finalists—now it is up to you to tell us which of these 69 rugs deserve the honor of being named Readers' Choice winners.

Review each of the winning rugs carefully and make your selections—1st, 2nd, and 3rd choice for each of the Commercial, Original, and Adaptation categories. Mark your choices on the attached ballot and be sure to mail it in before December 31, 2011.

Or for the first time, vote online. Go to *www.rughookingmagazine.com*, and look for the *Celebration* Readers' Choice link.

RHM appreciates the time you take to send in your Readers' Choice vote. Please help us honor the rug hooking artists represented within the pages of ***Celebration XXI*** by voting for your choice of the best of the best.

Sincerely,

Debra Smith

Editor

TEAR OFF HERE

READERS' CHOICE BALLOT

After reviewing all the rugs, fill out this ballot and mail it in to vote (Canadians, please use an envelope and your own postage). The winners of the Readers' Choice Contest will be announced in the June/July/August 2012 issue of *Rug Hooking* magazine. **Note: Ballots must be received by December 31, 2011.**

ORIGINAL RUG

1ST CHOICE

2ND CHOICE

3RD CHOICE

ADAPTATIONS

1ST CHOICE

2ND CHOICE

3RD CHOICE

COMMERCIAL RUG

1ST CHOICE

2ND CHOICE

3RD CHOICE

NAME

ADDRESS

CITY/STATE/ZIP PHONE NUMBER

RUG HOOKING MAGAZINE
5067 Ritter Rd.
Mechanicsburg, PA 17055-6921

Subscription Department
351 Riverside Industrial Parkway
Portland, ME 04103-1415

BUSINESS REPLY MAIL
FIRST-CLASS MAIL PERMIT NO. 22 PORTLAND ME

POSTAGE WILL BE PAID BY ADDRESSEE

Subscription Department
351 Riverside Industrial Parkway
Portland, ME 04103-1415

Sidewalk Jungle, 29³/₄″ x 40¹/₄″, ¹/₂″ cotton knit, silk weave, cotton weave.
Designed and hooked by Sheryl Alexander, Austin, Texas, 2010.

Merry Christmas, 21″ x 33″, #3-cut hand-dyed wool on burlap. *Adapted from a vintage Christmas card and hooked by Liz Smith, Upper Coverdale, New Brunswick, Canada, 2010.* PHOTO BY B. HIGGINS

Cat and Bird, 36" x 24", #4-, 5-, and 6-cut wool on linen. *Designed by Bev Conway;
hooked by Lonnie Williams, Austin, Texas, 2010.* PHOTO BY MARC BENNETT

1885 Horses, 47" x 17", #6-cut wool on monk's cloth. *Designed by Magdalena Briner/
Woolley Fox; hooked by Jan Winter, Hollywood, California, 2010.*

Imperfect Sunflowers, 48″ x 36″, #6-cut dyed and as-is wool on linen.
Designed and hooked by Melody Lavy, Waco, Texas, 2010. PHOTO BY JOE GRIFFIN

Jump for Joy, 24¹/₂″ x 36″,
#3- and 4-cut wool on linen. Adapted from a
photograph by Jason McLean and hooked by
Vicki Calu, Dublin, Pennsylvania, 2010.

PHOTO BY BILL BISHOP, IMPACT XPOSURES

Ginny B, 60″ round, #4- and 6-cut wool on monk's cloth. Designed by Jane Olson; hooked by Berniece C. Herron, Huntington Beach, California, 2010. PHOTO BY THE ENLARGER

A Single Flower, 11″ x 11″, #3-cut new wool, #8-cut new wool herringbone, and 2-ply yarn on linen. Designed and hooked by Heather Fox, New Denver, British Columbia, 2010.

Clovelly, 24″ x 34″, #3-, 4-, and 5-cut wool, flannel, and yarn on linen. Designed and hooked by Donalda (Donna) Gass, Prospect Bay, Nova Scotia, Canada, 2010.

Vermont, 54" x 31", #5-, 6-, and 7-cut wool on linen. Designed by Karen Kahle/
Primitive Spirit; hooked by Ann T. Sheedy, Waco, Texas, 2010. PHOTO BY JOE GRIFFIN

Petite Riviere,
36" x 27", #4-, 5-,
7-, and 8-cut wool,
roving, and yarn on
linen. Adapted from
a photo by Patricia
Monette and hooked
by Doris Eaton,
Crousetown, Nova
Scotia, Canada,
2010. PHOTO BY PETER
BARSS

the Traditional Rug:

The Exuberance of Orientals, Persians, and Florals

We were pleased to notice this year a larger than normal number of traditional-style rugs—those Persians, Orientals, and florals that are not for the faint of heart. Tackling one of these complex and demanding pieces requires a certain kind of courage and commitment. The results are spectacular, of course, and the feeling of accomplishment must be rewarding.

We are showing you a few more rugs—rugs that just missed the finalist list, but nevertheless are wonderful. Are traditional rugs making a comeback? Or is this only a momentary blip in the rug hooking world? We asked Jane McGown Flynn, pattern designer extraordinaire and granddaughter of Pearl McGown, for her thoughts on the resurgence of the traditional rug.

Far Left: *Birds of Sarouk, 40" x 60", #2-, 3-, and 4-cut wool on monk's cloth. Designed by Jane McGown Flynn; hooked by Lelia F. Ridgway, Honey Brook, Pennsylvania, 2010.* PHOTO BY BILL BISHOP, IMPACT XPOZURES

Left: *Zereh, 36" x 56", #4- and 6-cut wool on linen. Designed by Jane McGown Flynn; hooked by June Willingham, Monroe, Georgia, 2010.*

Rustic Wreath, 26" x 35",
#3- and 4-cut wool on linen.
Designed by Jane McGown
Flynn; hooked by Judith
Rippenstein, Fredericksburg,
Texas, 2010. PHOTO BY MARC
BENNETT, WHITE OAK STUDIO

Oriental, 28" x 53$\frac{1}{2}$",
#3-cut wool on linen. Designed
and hooked by Jaci Clements,
Dallas, Texas, 2010. PHOTO BY
LESLEY HINTON

New Fruit Bell Pull #218, 6" x 52", #3-cut wool on monk's cloth. Designed by Pearl McGown; hooked by Karen Haskett, Loveland, Colorado, 2010. PHOTO BY JAFE T. PARSONS

Jane McGown Flynn

Everyone in rug hooking who uses commercial patterns from pattern designers looks forward to seeing new designs each year. Developing new styles and patterns is important to every catalog business. But returning to the fabulous old standards of the past is a thrill for the designers.

Rug hooking designs run in cycles. As we are exposed to different styles, we are intrigued by the possibilities. Both traditional color plans and innovative color plans stimulate our creative juices and inspire us. I consider this cycle a very good thing. Imagine how long any single style or color plan would hold our attention if there were no possibility of change, surprise, or innuendo.

At the McGown Teacher Workshops, we invest a great deal of thought, time, and knowledge into improving our craft. Pearl McGown used to say, "If we have worked this hard to bring the art forward and refine it—in designs, color plans, dye methods, and tech-niques—why should we return to where it all started?" Perhaps she did not fully understand that design style is a choice—be it hooking with fine cuts, wide cuts, primitive hooking, or hooking with yarn.

Most designers will agree when I say that Orientals are the most difficult rugs to plan. There may be up to three medallions, which are complimented by several borders of varying widths. Perhaps it is the difficulty of these designs that attracted this year's *Celebration* participants to these challenging designs.

Persian Mini and *Jefferson Davis* were both designed in the 1950s by my grandmother. I am thrilled that they remain classics and continue to challenge rug hookers. Only time will tell if I have developed hooking designs that will become such classic pieces.

Thank you to everyone who continues to enjoy this fulfilling art form.

—Jane McGown Flynn
March 2011

Teec, 25¹/₂″ x 34″, #3-cut wool on monk's cloth. Designed by Jane McGown Flynn; hooked by Jeanne A. Sullivan, Annapolis, Maryland, 2009.

Pris' Padulas, 45″ x 34″, #4-cut wool on linen. Designed by Pris Buttler; hooked by Diane Luszcz, Hudson, New Hampshire, 2010.

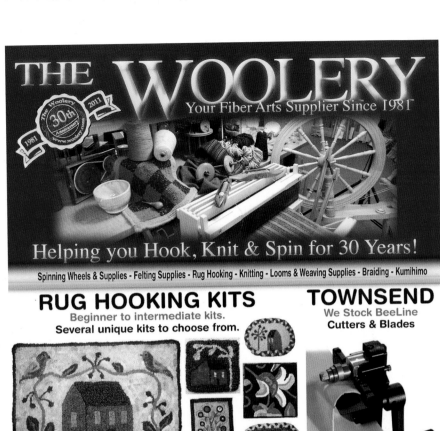

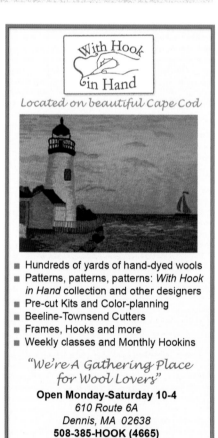